Troubles Don't Last,
YOU DO!

Persevering Through Adversity:
A Biblical Guide to Surviving Life's Hardships

KITT SWANSON

WESTBOW
PRESS®
A DIVISION OF THOMAS NELSON
& ZONDERVAN

All Scripture quotations, unless otherwise indicated, are taken from the Complete Word Study Bible, King James Version, copyright © 1998 by AMG Publishers. Used by permission of AMG Publishers. All rights reserved worldwide. www.amgpublishers.com.

WestBow Press books may be ordered through booksellers or by contacting:

WestBow Press
A Division of Thomas Nelson & Zondervan
1663 Liberty Drive
Bloomington, IN 47403
www.westbowpress.com
1 (866) 928-1240

ISBN: 978-1-5127-5201-4 (sc)
ISBN: 978-1-5127-5202-1 (hc)
ISBN: 978-1-5127-5200-7 (e)

Library of Congress Control Number: 2016913935

Print information available on the last page.

WestBow Press rev. date: 4/27/2017

The Lord is nigh unto them that are of a broken heart.

—Psalm 34:18

Contents

Dedication

I dedicate this book to the downtrodden. May you find comfort in Jesus, your present help in times of trouble (Psalm 46:1).

To Sis Sandra Bush and Bro Richard Prince, thank you for your prayers, encouraging words, and believing I could accomplish such a task.

Acknowledgments

A book such as this is never the product of one person. All praises go to God. He and His word were my inspiration in writing this book.

To the brokenhearted, thank you for letting me be a source of encouragement to you. May God give you a full measure of peace to share with others.

Last, many thanks to WestBow Press and its staff for making this book possible.

Introduction

Singleness ... marriage ... children ... job ... finances ... death troubles. These are the life cycle issues that catch God's people off guard and dash them against the rocks of hardship. Troubles arise and dissipate like the rise and fall of a heartbeat, but quandaries are an intricate part of a Christian's life (2 Timothy 3:12). God's people have both mountaintop and valley experiences. Hope in Christ helps believers to rise above their circumstances. Though the godly undergo suffering now, later they will enjoy glory with Jesus when He returns (Galatians 6:9):

> For I reckon that the sufferings of this present time
> are not worthy to be compared with the glory which
> shall be revealed in us (Romans 8:18).

God's people can expect to survive and thrive by standing on the Master's promises. The Bible doesn't promise believers an easy life, but it does tell them what to do when trials come:

> The righteous cry and the Lord heareth and delivered
> them out of all their troubles (Psalm 37:1).

Jesus understands every affliction and adversity His people endure (Hebrews 4:15). He was born human (John 1:1). However, because Jesus didn't sin, don't assume life was easy for Him (1 Peter 2:22–23). He faced a dreadful moment of separation from the Father. He suffered hatred, abuse, and the taunts of wicked men. His own people rejected Him, and religious leaders criticized Him. Yet Jesus continued to exhibit compassion throughout the scriptures. He didn't send away the woman with the issue of blood, and neither did He condemn the adulterous woman. Jesus offered an uplifting hand to the lame man, salve to the blind, and food to the multitude. He defeated death, and He is still standing.

Regardless of what you go through in this life, you too will withstand every storm you face if you remember … *troubles don't last, you do.*

Single and Hating It!

*Don't think of yourself as single; you are
romantically challenged.*
—Stephanie Piro

Another night of sobbing. You're lonely, angry, irritated, and emotional. There's no one to call; all your friends are on dates. Even the movie you're watching depresses you. You're single, and you hate being single. I got it.

The way you feel right now won't last. This happens to be your season to be single (Ecclesiastes 3:1). Jesus encourages you to stay strong during your times of loneliness. Let not your heart be troubled in such matters (John 14:1). He knows something you don't know—the future. Blissful joy awaits you, so dry your weeping eyes, blow your nose, and breathe. You've been given victory over your single struggles. Satan will send various types of joy-stealing attacks, but you will emerge victoriously. What God has for you is for you. No one or nothing can keep you from it. Don't allow disturbing thoughts such as, *No one wants me* or *I'm not good enough* crush your spirit. You are not defeated. If you need something to do other than boohooing, then carve out time to read God's Word; it will change your life, your circumstance, and your destiny. Allow God's Word to transform your thinking from negative assumptions to positive affirmations (Romans 12:2). If you want a change in your singleness, get out of the way and let the Master take control of your life. This battle you are fighting is not yours—it's the Lord's.

I can't keep you from the nemesis of loneliness, but I can share what I know about how to contend with it and help you avoid succumbing to the enemy of hopelessness. After all, *single troubles don't last, you do.* Rather than consuming hours of your day with thoughts of not having someone in your life, start a journal. It's great therapy during times of loneliness. It helps you dump your anxieties on paper and frees your mind to concentrate on godly matters. You can improve your self-image by shedding a few pounds, seeing a dermatologist for facial acne, or making an appointment for dental issues. Build your wardrobe with solids and pastels. Take a long-overdue trip, start a ministry, and get to know other singles. If you follow these steps, surely two results will follow:

1. You will emerge from your loneliness, crying, and depression. Job 5:19 says, "He shall deliver thee."

2. You will find love again. Peter says, "The Lord is not slack concerning his promise, as some men count slackness" (2 Peter 3:9).

Just in case you are wondering, God hears all your prayers (1 Peter 3:12). As a matter of fact, angels stand before God day and night, offering up your prayers as incenses before Him (Revelation 8:3). The passage reveals with ardent assurance that your prayer requests are not forgotten and that God will come to your rescue. Believers carry a vast weight in the spiritual realm. In that domain, at the mention of Jesus name every knee bows—in heaven, on earth, and under earth (Philippians 2:10). I tell you this because when you end your prayer with "in Jesus name," know that God will provide. All you need to do is wait. Paul confirms that everything that happens to you will work for your good (Romans 8:28). He isn't saying everything that happens to you is going to be good, but you are encouraged to trust God and resist handling matters your way (Proverbs 3:3–5). If you continue doing things your way, you are destined to remain in your situation until you learn to give your concerns over to the Master.

Furthermore, when you ask God to send you a mate, don't assume that perfect specimen will drop from heaven—*poof!*—right on your doorstep. Some things you have to do for yourself. James says faith without works is dead (James 2:18–26). For instance, you need a job to pay your bills. You petition God in prayer to give you a job. Sitting on the couch will not get you hired. You will have to exert an effort toward securing a job by creating a resumé or attending a job fair. Likewise, when you ask God for a mate, you need to visit places where a suitable mate can be found. Nightclubs are excluded. No suitable mate for a Child of God can be found in the vicinity of reveling and drinking. Great venues to meet godly singles would be at Christian seminars, conferences, and youth rallies. The Holy Spirit will help you: "Greater is he that is in you than he that is in the world" (1 John 4:4). You have everything inside you to find love.

Embrace Your Singleness

Accept your single status. Fighting it will only make the journey arduous. Choose between whining and complaining or trusting God, but you can't do both. God is not going to change your single status until you change your heart. Maya Angelou, an American author and poet, said, "If you don't like something, change it. If you can't change it, change your attitude."[1] Paul advises us that God's Word will transform us (Romans 12:2). James divulges that the Word of God is a reflection device. It is used as you would a mirror, and you should pay close attention to what it reveals (James 1:25). The Bible is congruent to an annual physical checkup. A physical checkup is a preventive measure to screen for sickness and disease. Use the Bible to screen for sin (2 Corinthians 13:5). When an area of sin is revealed, repent of it. Also, eradicate relationship baggage prior to forming a bond with someone else. The unhealthy residue of a failed relationship going into another relationship is disastrous to your mental psyche. *How can you move forward tied to your past?* Furthermore, a pity party is not allowed. Embrace your singleness; It's temporary. Refusing to wait on God tells Him you have no faith that He can deliver on prayers you've uttered to Him (Hebrews 11:6). Do not waste another moment in a pool of tears because you have no love in your life. Love yourself first. True love isn't euphoric—it's a deliberate choice.

---

[1] Sury, Vidya. Phenomenal Woman Maya Angelous Inspiring Quotes. 28 May 2014.
http://vidyasury.com/2014/05/maya-angelou-inspiring-quotes.html

If you haven't already, you will have some lonely days. Jesus, the Son of God, had them (Matthew 27:46). The apostle Paul had them (2 Timothy 4:9–22). This isn't some new phenomenon. God recognizes loneliness. He saw it in the garden when He noticed Adam watching all the animals with mates. At that point, God said, "It is not good for the man to be alone" (Genesis 2:18). He sprang into action and created an amazing creature from Adam's rib—his soulmate, Eve (Genesis 2:21–24). God gave Adam a mate, and He will give you one too.

There is a myth that if you are single, something is wrong with you. Since when has singleness become unpopular? You're not weird because you don't follow society's script of having someone in your life. Being alone isn't a disease—it's an opportunity to get to know yourself better. Artist Brendan Francis says, "At the innermost core of all loneliness is a deep and powerful yearning for union with one's lost self."[2] We all agonize over understanding and loving ourselves. It's easier to seek out others to love us rather than dealing with ourselves. You are to love others as you love yourself, but if you cannot love yourself, then draw near to Jesus (Matthew 22:39). He will show you how. The writer of Hebrews tells us how to draw near to Jesus. Hebrews 10:22–23 says:

> Let us draw near with a true heart in full assurance of faith, having our hearts sprinkled from an evil conscience, and our bodies washed with pure water. Let us hold fast the profession of our faith without wavering; for he is faithful that promised; and let us

---

[2] Jim, Big. When Loneliness Sets In? 14 Years ago. http://www.jehovahs-witness.com/topic/6861/when-loneliness-sets?page=1&size=20.html.

consider one another to provoke unto love and to good works.

Notice there are three "let us" statements that stand out in the above passage: (1) "Let us draw near." Don't drift away from your hope. (2) "Let us hold fast" to our faith. Don't waver when discomforting situations arise. And (3) "Let us consider" one another. Encourage other singles through their loneliness with the comfort you received from the one who comforted you during your isolated times (2 Corinthians 1:4).

Don't underestimate the power of God. He is able to bring about a change in your single status. For this to occur, you must keep your eyes on Him. Stop fixating on a mate; God's grace is covering your desolate heart. Turn your singleness over to the Lord; you will be dating before you know it.

God's Impatient Child

Nowadays, people want everything now. They will purchase Wi-Fi instead of waiting to get to a free Wi-Fi location, and they will pay the enormous prices at the movie theater instead of waiting for the movie to air on Netflix. At what point do you start waiting on the Lord? Although we reside in a society wherein everyone is impatient and wants fast responses, God doesn't function that way. It doesn't matter how lonely you are or how much praying you do; everything is in God's own timing (Isaiah 55:7–8). God is in the heavens and does what He wants (Psalm 115:3). He will not scurry His timetable to send you a mate without grooming you for such a venture. Furthermore, refrain from treating your prayer life like a vending machine in which you deposit a prayer, make a selection, and expect an immediate response. You've heard the old adage, "He may not come when you want Him, but He's always on time." That's how God performs. Despite the views of some, God is concerned about your loneliness.[3] Just as God watches the sparrow when it falls, surely God sees your lonely heart and knows your needs. Before the creation of the world, God had you in mind (Ephesians 1:4). He knew every struggle and every difficulty you would face in this life. He has equipped you for each unforeseen event Satan would fling at you.

God never said the single life was going to be easy. He did promise not to abandon you in your hour of need. Keep pressing toward your prize until your victory is won. Keep fighting, keep praying, keep fasting, keep believing, keep interceding, and keep trusting because it's not over until God says it's over. You may feel like you cried your last tear, but God still has the final say. Take to heart what Jesus taught on a Galilean mountainside. He taught various subjects everyone understood as significant life advice:

> Therefore, take no thought, saying, what shall we eat? or, what shall we drink? or, wherewithal shall we be clothed? For after all these things do the Gentiles seek; for your heavenly Father knoweth that you have need of all these things. But seek ye first the kingdom of God, and his righteousness; and all these things shall be added unto you (Matthew 6:31–33).

---

[3] Uygur, Cenk. God Doesn't Care About Us. 25 May 2011. Blog. 27 June 2015. http://www.huffingtonpost.com/cenk-uygur/god-doesnt-care-about-us_b_7840.html.

God's panoramic view stretches beyond your comprehension and into your circumstance. Do not mistake what is happening to you as a lack of understanding by God. Your single status is not by happenstance. You are right where God wants you, receiving a lesson in perseverance. I know how difficult it can get to be patient when you want something desperately. You fall on your knees repeatedly concerning a mate. At times, you feel like God is not listening. The fact of the matter is, He is listening. He's not like a friend who hears only parts of your conversation. God hears everything. God is leading you through your maze of loneliness. All will work out in God's timing like a cake at the end of its cycle in the oven (Romans 8:38). When you bake a cake, you don't blend all the ingredients in a bowl and then eat the batter. You put the mixture in a pan and place the pan in the oven to cook. As the batter reaches cooking temperature, you savor the aroma. When the cake rises to the top of the pan and a golden brown color appears, you retrieve that delicious mixture from the oven, let it cool, then top it with icing. Thereafter, you pounce on that vanilla-smelling sweetness like a cat. Likewise, in order for the gift of your mate to be perfect, you must wait for the Master's perfect timing (Psalm 40:1). Then, and only then, will you be able to pounce on the blessing God has for you.

God knows how to give good gifts (James 1:17). Your mate will be better than you could ever imagine (Ephesians 3:20). You may hate being single right now, but this won't last. You will come through it like an Olympic gold winner.

Secret Admirer

You are so busy seeking love, did you know you had a secret admirer? God has a crush on you, and it's not a secret. He's a master at revealing His intentions toward you. His strong feelings for you led Him to sacrifice His only Son for your sins. At night when you're crying over the mate you lost or want, God is holding you. He bottles your tears as souvenirs (Psalm 56:8). If someone did that today, you would call him a stalker. Well, God is your stalker. He's cradling you in His arms while you sleep. He listens intently to your prayers. He's an avid listener of your dinnertime discussions. God allows you to talk about your day and then gives you big hug, while whispering in your ear, *Everything will be all right.* Yet you reject all His loving attempts to bring you closer to Him because you desire a human love. *How do you think that makes Him feel?* He feels like you do—abandoned and alone. God empathizes with you and knows your intimate desires. He is personally in your life. He knows how many hairs are on your head (Matthew 10:30). Your painful longing for a mate won't last because God is there.

When your skies look gray and you're on the verge of a loneliness breakdown, hold onto your faith. Don't give up on God (Job 14:14). Everyone else may have failed you, but God won't. He is a faithful mate who will never leave you (Isaiah 54:5). When loneliness overwhelms you, talk to the Father (1 Peter 5:7). Although you feel like you are slipping away, the Spirit inside you is renewed daily with hope and fortitude (2 Corinthians 4:16). It's gaining strength and momentum with each prayer you utter. There's a power in prayer.

Don't allow Satan to deceive you into thinking you need a mate right now because everyone else has one. He comes this way because he knows if a Christian recognizes a suggestion of evil coming from him, he won't get anywhere close, so Satan hides himself behind enticing thoughts to make his trap attractive. *I just want to wrap him in honey and lick it off. I'm a leg and breast man.* He makes you think you came up with those thoughts. When you learn to recognize his approach, then half of your battle will be won. Dig your faith heels in the sand, and tell Satan to get behind you (Matthew 16:23). Your single troubles won't last, but as a child of God you will.

Troubles in this life are unavoidable (Job 14:1). If you want to enter the kingdom of God, you must go through hardship. Reject the urge to throw in the white flag. The Lord will deliver you from your loneliness when He feels you are ready. I realize it's a struggle to do good in a world where wrong is morally acceptable, but it's not impossible (Luke 1:37). I sense you are tired of wasting your weekends in isolation and long to be someone's plus one. Keep hope alive. The entity that conquers loneliness is faith (1 John 5:4). Hold onto your faith. Guard your mind and heart at all times against Satan and his gambits. He is out to destroy you, which leads me to the discussion of dating sites (1 Peter 5:8). Stay clear of dating sites. Online coaches will convince you that the mate of your dreams is obtainable. You tell them about yourself and the person you would like to meet, and they will assist you in filling out an online systematic profile application to meet your mate. If it were that easy, you would have found a mate long before now. Deal with your loneliness instead of avoiding it. Finding a suitable mate is going to take some time. Don't rush the process. Haven't you already seen the outcome of not waiting on God from your former relationships?

If you pleaded for God to send you a mate and have not received one, it could be that your motive for having a partner may not be in alignment with God's will (James 4:3). Have you thought about why you want a mate? Are you seeking a companion to marry for security or to satisfy a sexual desire? Deciding to have a consort is an important life decision that shouldn't be taken haphazardly. You can't go by your inclinations or emotions in this vital decision. Take your time in your selection, and allow God to navigate you to the mate of your dreams. Choose carefully and wisely; your eternity depends on it.

Avoidable Mistakes

Years ago, singles courted to find marriage companions. Now they date to satiate their own interests—to kill time, requite a past relationship, escape loneliness, or just acquire sex. Self-control is a difficult trait to manage—for everyone, especially after indulging in sexual activity. Spending meaningful one-on-one time with someone without having sexual desires is arduous. Affections play a chief part in relationships. Combine that with singles' challenges and you get frustration. Try to look for someone to connect with on a spiritual level. Your single challenges are more manageable when you both have heavenly goals. Also, you are not bizarre or eccentric because you haven't had a date in the last three to six months. You are showing others how serious you are about dating. However, the stress of not having a date may cause you to lose your objectivity. Here are few recommendations to keep you on track:

- Although dating can alleviate loneliness, desperation dating compromises who you are as a Christian. Don't trade happiness and peace of mind for sex, material prosperity, or emotional dependence. Doing this is just a temporal Band-Aid for loneliness. The emptiness will remain until you fill yourself with God.

- Don't date people you have no interest in marrying. I'm talking about the ones you're not attracted too but hang out with to keep from being home alone.

- Don't settle for a person you know God won't be pleased with. Be meticulous when finding a mate; after all, you are a child of God. Keep realistic expectations; don't look for the perfect mate. Only God is perfect.

- Honor your body with purity. Show your commitment to God by waiting to have sex. Don't use sex as a weapon or as a means to possess someone. Your body is the temple of the Holy Spirit (1 Corinthians 3:16–17). It's your obligation to protect this gift of intimacy until you are married. God will bless you for it.

- Don't brood, pout, and complain about your singleness; it's pushing away family, friends, and potential dates.

- Family members and friends will eventually introduce you to one of their acquaintances or someone they feel is suitable or someone who has similar struggles as you. On your first date with this person, please don't tell your life story. In other words, don't put all your cards on the table, hoping to weed out any uncommitted mates because you've been hurt in the past. Too much information scares off potential companions. Keep mystery and intrigue in your arsenal.

- Say the lighting in the restaurant is low, soft music is playing in the background, and your date tells you things you want to hear. Slow down. Don't start planning a future with this person in your head. It's only the first date. This could be an agent of Satan coming into your life as an opportunist to lead you into spiritual decay (1 Corinthians 15:33).

- Rushing into anything is never good. Stop leaping blindly into relationships. Take the time to assess your last relationship. Work through the emotional, verbal, and physical baggage you are carrying. Don't ignore those feelings and go off seeking new love. You will never find the right person until you settle your unresolved issues.

- Talk to God about your single status. Ask Him to guide you to the person He wants you to have. Keep prayer on your dating checklist.

- Say you prayed for a mate for weeks, months, or years and God still hasn't answer your prayers. Remember who God is. He is grooming someone very special for you who will exceed all your expectations (Ephesians 3:20). Wait on the Lord! God's timetable is different from yours, and He is the only one who knows what's best for you (Isaiah 55:7–8).

- Stop falling for people you think will be successful. For example, if you meet a person who shines shoes, but has the dream of becoming a doctor, don't see yourself with a doctor; see yourself with a shoe shiner. It's not to say the person won't become a doctor, just don't get involved with someone because of future aspirations.

Appearances

Looks matter. Don't fool yourself into thinking you don't care how the other person looks; that's the loneliness talking. If your date is not easy on the eyes, instinctively you will come up with excuses to avoid family and friends' ridiculing and drop your date faster than Domino's pizza delivery.

Solomon, the wisest man who ever lived, said, "Beauty is vain, but one that fears the Lord shall be praised" (Proverbs 31:30). A godly mate is beautiful inside and out, and one that fears the Lord. An eye-catching mate is a worldly mate who is great to parade around your friends in the beginning. At some point, that handsome or beautiful mate might have you starving yourself or losing yourself in vain practices. What will happen if an accident mutilates your dazzling or attractive mate? Do you stick with the person, or do you bow out of the relationship gracefully? If you bow out, what does that say about you? Appearances are deceiving.

God taught Samuel a valuable lesson on appearances. God sent Samuel to anoint the new king of Israel, but He didn't tell Samuel who to anoint. Samuel thought he would recognize the person by his appearance, but God told Samuel, "Not to look on his countenance or on the height of his stature. The Lord seeth not as man seeth; for man looketh on the outward appearance, but the Lord looketh on the heart" (1 Samuel 16:7). Beauty doesn't last no matter what you do to preserve that youthful look.

Godly singles look beyond appearances because looks don't last; you do.

Unequally Yoked

Are you seeking a godly mate? Don't form a relationship, temporarily or permanently, with unbelievers (2 Corinthians 6:14). Such a relationship leads to a compromise of your faith and could jeopardize your witnessing. You can't please an unbeliever and keep your godly standards; it doesn't work. Similarly, you can't go to places unbelievers go and maintain your Christian morals. This concept is a good example of light and darkness; both can't occupy the same space; neither can a relationship with a believer and nonbeliever survive. There will be a constant tug of war. What can a nonbeliever do for you but lure you into a love affair based on material possessions? Luke wrote, "Take heed and beware of covetousness; for a man's life consists not in the abundance of the things which he possesses" (Luke 12:14). It is not about what your potential mate owns that should concern you; it's who owns your potential mate. There are two masters (Matthew 6:24); which one is your potential mate serving?

Control Your Single Destiny

Your destiny is larger than you can comprehend. Don't allow Satan to steal it from you. He is like a time traveler who goes back into time to sabotage your bright future by tricking you into being impatient. You are the keeper of your Christian destiny. You determine your dating road. For example, if you're making all the calls after a date, and you rarely hear from the other person, let that person go. If you're making the plans and spending all the money, let that person go. That person doesn't understand oneness. Oneness is defined as two people coming together toward a common goal. Look for someone who will be with you during the good and bad times, not someone who will drive you to the next block and drop you off as soon as the relationship doesn't go as planned. You want someone who is trustworthy, not a liar; stable, not imbalanced; dependable, not erratic. And most of all you need a committed person in your life who loves the Lord. Surrender your singleness to God. Start controlling your singleness today by getting to know God. He has a promising future in store for you (Jeremiah 29:11).

Your singleness won't last, but you as a child of God will!

Married, but Miserable!

Marriage is not supposed to make you feel good,
or make you feel miserable. Marriage is just
supposed to make you feel.
—*Gloria Naylor*

This isn't your typical "how-to-save your marriage" chapter. There are plenty of counselors and self-help books available to coach you into reconciliation. My task is to encourage you to keep the faith during your marital squalls. Your disagreements and conflicts may seem like an eternity, but they won't last. You will outshine every obstacle Satan places before you and your spouse (Isaiah 54:17). Your job is to stand still and watch the salvation of the Lord (Exodus 14:13). You have Jesus, who says no one will snatch you out of His hand (John 10:28).

Marriage undergoes difficulties and comes with a mixture of blessings and trials, highs and lows. Appreciate the highs, weather the lows, and treasure the rest. It doesn't matter how long you have been married, the ups and downs will come. Still, the Master wants you to have a blessed, peaceful, happy, and fulfilled marriage. You can achieve such a felicity with Jesus's help. When you have problems in your marriage, He is willing to take your burdens and make them His own, but first you have to give them to Him (Matthew 28:11). He will sustain you and not allow you to fall because He cares just that much (Psalm 55:22). Every evil thing that threatens your marriage, He will use it for your benefit. Further, Jesus promises your trials will be bearable and will make a way of escape for you (1 Corinthians 10:13). First you will have to look for the opening.

Continue to pray. Prayer and fasting relocate you into a firm position to speak to the struggles in your marriage. Don't allow Satan to sway you from your position of faith. And if you are in a season of refining, lean in. God is about to do something extraordinary with you and your spouse. If Satan can get you to move away from God, you're in an awful predicament. He wants to destroy your marriage. Walk by faith in your circumstance. Take a strong stance against the devil's cunning and deceitful tactics by putting on the full armor of God listed in Ephesian 6. Do not lose hope when troubles surround you. Ambivalence and distrust can fill you with anxiety. However, your anxiety will dissipate when you keep your eyes on the Author and Finisher of your faith (Hebrews 12:2). Be assured that what God has promised He is able to perform. You will survive your marriage struggles. God's work is perfect, and His ways are just. He will deliver you from all your troubles (Psalm 50:15). No matter what you encounter, He'll bring you through.

Energize yourself with God's Word. Think on things that are positive and good (Philippians 4:8). Be careful how you walk in your marriage. Satan strategically place landmines in your path to divert your attention from God. So when you mess up, immediately ask for forgiveness. Repent. God will iron out the wrinkles of your marriage. It's not easy to navigate through discomfort. Pain blinds you. Therefore, when you get caught up in your own struggles, seek God's help first, rather than trying to work things out yourself (Proverbs 3:5). Avoid any thought of taking matters in your own hands. You are moving where God doesn't want you to go.

It happened to Abraham and Sarah (Genesis 16:1–16). Abraham sought God about which of his servants he would pass on his inheritance. God previously told Abraham that he would have an heir, one from his own seed, not from another man (Genesis 15:4). Abraham trusted God enough to leave his home in Ur, but he didn't trust God enough to give him a child in his old age. *Aren't we like that too—we trust God in some things, but in others we lose faith (Genesis 16:2–3). With God, it's all or nothing (Matthew 6:24).* Because of Abraham's lack of faith, he allowed his wife to talk him into having a child with another woman, Hagar (Genesis 1:1-3). I don't know how much prodding was done; I just know that a happy home was destroyed because Abraham and Sarah didn't wait on God. Don't make the same mistake. Wait on the Lord!

Furthermore, you may want revenge or to walk away from the marriage because your spouse violated your trust; however, I encourage you to walk with the Holy Spirit and not let your unfortunate circumstance lead you to do something you will regret later (1 John 1:7). Stop magnifying your marital troubles; magnify God, who is bigger than your circumstance. This is no easy task; believe me, I know. However, God wants you to trust Him (Hebrews 11:6). Trusting God means that you trust in His plan for you and your marriage. There's nothing too hard for Him to handle (Genesis 18:14). He has your marriage and all its struggles in His sight. Besides, this isn't the first spat between you and your spouse, and it won't be the last. Something else will surely come along and tip the scales of life, but God will be there for you (Hebrews 13:5). He can and will save your marriage, if you allow Him.

Imagine a time when you were a newlywed. You approached the idea of marriage with vigor and eagerness. You and your spouse were polite and thoughtful toward one another. You tiptoed around each other so as not to cause a commotion. With time, care and consideration disappeared. Boredom crept in soon after. A dull daily routine began to kill your marriage. Both of you initiated decisions without discussing the matter with one another. Thus, feelings of resentment grew. One's own self-interest became more important than the spouse's emotional state. Soon after, you and your spouse drifted apart—in intimacy, communication, and common interests.

God's prescription for a healthy marriage is unity (Genesis 2:24). It's a partnership. It's oneness. It takes two people to make a marriage work. King Solomon wrote, "Two are better than one because if one falls, the other will give him a hand; but unhappy is the man who is by himself, because he has no helper" (Ecclesiastes 4:9). That scripture doesn't say three is better than two. There's no room for additional people in a marriage. God intended for two people to become as one. No other should join that union. Therefore, when there's a disagreement between you and your spouse, consult each other, not your best friend, not your parents, not your cousin or your siblings. The matter is between you and your spouse. When there are other people involved in your marriage, your troubles triple.

Never allow anyone else in your marriage. It doesn't matter if it is family or otherwise. If you need an extra person in your marriage, get a therapist. Marriage is a gift from God. However, sometimes even the greatest of gifts in life are not appreciated the way they should be. Don't take one another for granted. Don't keep old emotions bottled up from a previous relationship. Give those things to the Lord. The trouble in your marriage won't last if both parties submit to the will of the Father.

> As we have therefore opportunity, let us do good unto all men, especially unto them who are of the household of faith (Galatians 6:10).

Miserable

As we say in the military, your spouse wasn't issued to you. You chose the person you married. Despite the many warnings from friends and family, you married your spouse anyway. The Holy Spirit urged you to step back and ponder your decision. You recognized the warning signs, but you chose to marry despite them. You probably thought that if you believed hard enough, the good would conquer the bad. Now you cry and sob nearly every day, your marriage worsens, and you're miserable.

One thing worse than a miserable person is a miserable married person. No one gets married to be lonely and unhappy. You marry to share life's adventures and to be loved. You had hoped your spouse would be your lifelong companion, someone who would save you from loneliness, yet here you are feeling helpless and alone. This

21

feeling is from Satan. His strategy is to divide and conquer, and to place a wedge between you and your spouse. Don't allow that to happen, and don't pretend you're not having struggles in your marriage. Hurt, left unattended for a long time, builds resentment and breeds separation and loneliness. Whatever hurt you've endured, forgive your spouse as God has forgiven you (Matthew 6:14). All have sinned and come short of God's glory (Romans 3:23). No one is perfect but God. Spend time together talking about your issues in a nonthreatening environment. Go to the beach or take a walk on the pier. Go back to your dating days, hold hands, or snuggle on the couch. Physical closeness tends to lead to emotional closeness.

What you don't want is to retreat to your neutral corners; that's a haven for the devil to play with your mind and create a bigger divide between you and your spouse. This kind of reaction gives Satan a stronger foothold in your marriage. It opens the door for another person to join the marriage. Furthermore, don't sweep your martial conflicts under a rug, and don't run into the arms of another. Deal with your issues. If you can't achieve this task alone, get a counselor. There will be times when your spouse doesn't want anyone to know you are having troubles. This is the time to seek marriage counseling. Go alone if you must, but please get help. Most importantly, plead your case before the Father in fasting and prayer. He will give you clarity.

Sometimes we are miserable because of the choices we made while dating—those choices spill over into our marriages. There was a younger sister named Cathy at a church I attended years ago who settled down with a handsome young preacher named Thomas. (These names are made up to protect the innocent.) They met at a church conference, and Thomas was a good catch to any sister who could land him. *What sister wouldn't want to be with a preacher?* Anyway, Thomas was an eloquent speaker and skilled at explaining scriptures to the novice. He always gave his undivided attention to those in need. The congregation hired him as its youth minister because he had a way with the teens. They thought Thomas was so *cool.* They would call him day or night for advice. Cathy knew someday he would be a wonderful father. Several times she mentioned starting a family, but each time he said that it wasn't a good time because so many people needed him.

Little by little their marriage took a turn for the worst. Thomas started coming home at two o'clock in the morning, and on other occasions, he wouldn't come home at all. When he did come home, Cathy would ask him where he had been, but he'd just walk past her, without any explanation, and get into bed. Cathy prayed for their marriage. One night she heard sounds coming from the living room. Fearing there was an intruder, she grabbed the baseball bat near their bed. She went to investigate, only to find Thomas and a young woman acting inappropriately. She confronted him. He slapped Cathy in front of his guest and began to choke her. He told her never to speak about the incident to anyone, and if she did that he would kill her.

Thomas continued his lustful behavior, and Cathy kept her mouth shut for many years. At church she pretended that Thomas was someone else so her smile would be genuine.

When Thomas went out of town with the youth group, Cathy visited Tracey, another Christian sister she admired. Tracey had been incarcerated for stabbing her minister husband to death. No one knew what set her off to commit such a crime; she never talked about it. *Ministers are human, and they struggle with sins too. They are not exempt from working out their soul salvation with trembling and fear (Philippians 2:12). Many of them need exposing. Their shame could save their souls and marriages. That is the beauty of repentance. Godly women keep silent to mimic the quiet spirit Peter talks about (1 Peter 3:4).*

After Tracey listened attentively to Cathy's story, there was a long period of silence. Then Tracey whispered, "The grass is not always greener on the other side, is it?" Meaning that marriage is not a fairy tale that lasts forever. At that point, Cathy remembered the scripture, "Trust in the LORD with all your heart; and lean not unto your own understanding, in all thy ways acknowledge God, and he shall direct your paths" (Proverbs 3:5). Cathy hadn't waited on God to select her mate. Rather, she saw a minister with great potential and fell in love with his status. The Bible tells us to look at what God looks at: "Not to look on his countenance or on the height of his stature. The Lord seeth not as man seeth; for man looketh on the outward appearance, but the Lord looketh on the heart" (1 Samuel 16:7).

Although both marriages ended tragically, my heart leaps with exceeding joy to know both women are Christians and their marital troubles didn't last. They found strength and peace in the Lord.

If you're struggling in your marriage, there's a demonic element present. Your inner turmoil is a struggle between good and evil. If your optimism and hopefulness are not the same and you can't shake it, or you feel an unusual jealousy leading to rage, cast all your cares upon Lord. Spring into action to rid your marriage of this evil presence. Give your heart to Lord. Repent of personal sins, and ask your spouse to forgive you. Break ties from people causing issues in your marriage. Predetermine to live holy. Make your best-read novel the Bible. Pray against any activity Satan throws at your marriage.

You may know not if it's a spiritual fight or a bad day at first. As your marriage problems worsen, you will know it's a spiritual fight. Satan is determined to destroy the home. Lay all your marital troubles downs at the altar. God keeps all His promises. He did it in the Old Testament, and He is still keeping them right now (2 Peter 3:9). By continuing to be Christlike, you are showing your mate a living demonstration of the gospel of Jesus Christ (1 Peter 3:1–5).

If you have done all you can for your marriage, then live a life for Jesus. Walk as a redeemed soldier with your hand in the Lord's hand. You represent heaven when you do good and suffer for it (1 Peter 4:16). Suffering provides fresh insights into the gospel. It unveils why Jesus died on the cross and your pathway to righteousness. That path is where Jesus is sheltering you with His mighty arms right now. Cry, scream, or even call a friend, but know, "Joy comes in the morning" (Psalm 30:5). All marriages have vicissitudes. Think back to your last disagreement. That feat wasn't settled through your wisdom; it was, "because of the Lord's great love you were not consumed, for His compassion never fails. They are new every morning; great is His faithfulness" (Lamentation 3:22–23).

There's peace in the midst of your storm when your eyes are on the Lord (Isaiah 26:3). Joseph thought all hope was gone when his brothers sold him to a traveling caravan (Genesis 37:23–28); nonetheless, he became Pharaoh's second-in-command. My point is that God didn't leave or forsake Joseph, and God won't leave or forsake you. He's right where you need Him during times of marriage trials. One thing about God, He doesn't change (Malachi 3:6). Take comfort in knowing that.

In the midst of your marriage problems, you may ask yourself, "Where is God in all this?" Sometimes God allows trials to get you to relinquish your stubborn ways to His will. Don't be mistaken, He hears your prayers; however, He is waiting for you to hear Him. Close your eyes and look back over your life. Hasn't God delivered you through some amazing situations? This trial is no different. Trials are a natural part of a Christian maturing. "All that live godly in Christ Jesus will suffer persecution" (1 Timothy 3:12).

Jeremiah, the prophet, knew all too well about adversity and depression. Just like you, he reached a low point in his life. He prayed to God, and his prayers recoiled to earth. He remembered every painful event in his life. Yet, Jeremiah made it through his trials by remembering his Hope (Jeremiah 29:11). Hold onto your Hope, and you will make it through your hardships. Your marital troubles won't last, you will—as long as you stay close to the Master.

The Best Role Model for Your Marriage

The best role model for your marriage is God and His love for sinners (John 3:16). In the midst of your sins, God commenced operation *Redeem and Love.* He sent His only Son to earth to die for your sins (Romans 5:8). Let's go back to Calvary. Listen to the pounding sounds of nails as wicked men drove them into the hands and feet of Jesus. Listen to His bones crack as the men raised the wooden beam up to the sky for all to see, then let it drop into the deep hole they dug. Remember the pain and anguish Jesus suffered. God's Son died a bloody death. Would you send your child to die for people you knew would willfully sin after you sent him? It seems pointless. Yet, God personifies love. His very nature screams love (1 John 4:8). Did you know God loves you with an everlasting love (Jeremiah 31:3)? There is nothing you can do to stop Him from loving you. Similarly, Jesus epitomizes the same kind of love. Christ loved the church so much that He died for it (Ephesian 5:25).

Emulate God and Jesus's love if you want marital bliss. Love is kind, not rude, nor does it seek to have its way. It's not easily provoked either (1 Corinthians 13:4-5). Jesus didn't just say, "Okay Father, I'll go down and die for the mortals." He put His words into action (Philemon 1:21). You and your spouse stood before God and man vowing to love one another. It's time to put your words into action. Whatever sin crept into your marriage can be defeated with prayer and two willing people kneeling before the Master (Philippians 3:6–7). This struggle in your marriage is only temporary and it won't last, but you will with the help of God.

Keep Your Eyes on Jesus

Before you hit that, "Dear God, I can't handle this anymore. My spouse is driving me crazy!" boiling point, look to Jesus. The very area of your life that seems impossible to manage is possible through Jesus' strength (Luke 1:37). Yes, trials are annoying and irritating.

Yes, they come at times when you are not ready for them. Just because you're a Christian doesn't mean you won't have adversities, nor are you equipped to prevent bad things from happening in your life. Remember, it's not the storm that's important; it's how you handle your storm that shows your true character.

Run to Jesus when your storms are raging. Jesus tells you to, "Let not your heart be troubled" (John 14:27). Oftentimes He allows the circumstances of life change you into a Christlike specimen. This wouldn't have happened on its own. God had to allow hardships to metamorphose you into the person He knows you are capable of becoming. Take this opportunity to embrace your transformation. Your difficulties may not seem like a gift from God, but they are. It's beyond the pain that you see the big picture. Amazement is in your future.

> Blessed is the man that endureth temptation, for when he is tried, he shall receive the crown of life, which the Lord has promised to them that love him (James 1:12).

Stay strong. Stand tall. Your reward is around the corner. Your ordeal is just a speed bump in the road, a low-raised ridge across a roadway. You slow down enough to drive over it, and then you press the gas of life toward your goal. Your speed bumps are temporary (James 4:14). With prayer and patience, your marriage will be back on track. Spousal troubles don't last; you the Christian do.

Here are a few words of encouragement to keep your marriage aligned with God's word:

1. Love God first; then it will be easier for you to love your spouse (Matthew 6:33).

2. Pray with and for your spouse. Prayer binds your hearts into one common goal.

3. Emulate Christ's love for His Bride—the church. This kind of love is what it takes to make a marriage work—a sacrificial love (Ephesians 5:23–25).

4. Keep in mind that you are not perfect. It makes forgiving your spouse easier. Keep in memory that God forgave you (Matthew 6:14).

5. You're one in the Lord. Let no man separate what God has joined together (Matthew 19:6).

6. Remember true happiness comes from God, not from your spouse. Keep your eyes on God if you want to be happy (Psalm 121:1).

7. Don't put your faith in your spouse; put your faith in God, who is perfect in all things (Matthew 5:48).

8. Use God's love as a model for your marriage.

9. Keep the promises you made to each other at the altar.

10. When you have a disagreement or argument, remember Jesus is in the room.

11. Be satisfied with the mate God blessed you with. When times get tough, don't run into the arms of another; work with the mate you have.

In order for marriage to work, you can't be selfish. Two people going separate ways can never obtain oneness as God intends. Marriage takes oneness. Don't have the *me-first* mentality. Satan uses egocentric desires to kill a marriage, and oftentimes he is successful. Don't let selfishness be the reason your marriage doesn't work. It's the job of both partners to ensure fulfillment in a marriage. Also, consider the singles and new converts in church who are observing your marriage. Many singles opt out of marriage based on marriage performances they see among Christian couples.

This "How Come" poem sums it up:

How Come

How come when there's a problem between you and I,
we can't seem to solve it, neither do we try.
We'll sing praises to God and even kneel for prayer,
yet when it comes to true repentance, our hearts just aren't there.

How come we hurt each other so?
Couldn't we just let it go?
Revenge never solved a thing.
Try denying yourself, try love this spring.

How come we say we're Christians
when we don't live that way.
Others see us fussing and fighting
and doing evil day after day.

How come new converts come and go?
What makes them lose their glow?
They come for eternal life,
but we give them hatred and strife.

Keep killing one another with evil words,
soon the world will see
what kind of Christian we really are
and what we turned out to be.

Last question, this I must know,
how come when you were lost,
you didn't stay that way?
What made you seek a new boss?
Were you promised earthly things?
Is that why you stepped away from the cross?

Please wake up before it's too late and you're at heaven's door.
Seek the God of heaven, and beg for His mercy once more.
It's not too late to get it straight and be among the saved.
Keep the faith; hold your course, God's on the way!

Don't become self-centered, and don't allow yourself to get in the way of righteous living in your marriage (2 Timothy 3:1–4).

Be like-minded, having the same love, being of one accord, of one mind. Let nothing be done through selfish ambition or conceit, but in lowliness of mind let each esteem others better than himself (Philippians 2:2–3).

Make the best out of your marriage. Your marriage troubles won't last; you and your spouse will get through this. You will tell your success story to your grandchildren. Keep heaven in your viewfinder.

With Kids and Frustrated

And in the end, it's not the years in your life that count.
It's the life in your years.
—Abraham Lincoln

"Stop pulling your sister's hair!" "Put that rock down!" "Keep your feet on the floor!" One of the most unpleasant encounters parents confront is a child's behavior problems. Child behavior is perplexing and not easily noticed, like an injury or sickness. When your child's disposition changes, rely on the Lord (Proverbs 3:3–5). Face each day with hope instead of drudgery. Do you remember why you wanted your bundle of joy? I asked several parents why they chose to have children. These were their responses:

- "I needed a purpose in life."

- "I came from a fairly decent-size family, so I wanted to have what I grew up with."

- "I wanted a family, no special reason."

- "To carry on the family name."

- "I absolutely *love* children! Ever since I was a little girl playing house and being the oldest in my family and cousins, I enjoyed making them laugh and playing games with them.

- "I wanted to feel closer to my spouse."

- "When I get older, I want someone to take care of me."

- "My biological clock was ticking."

Many parents aspire to give their children every advantage they didn't have. It's natural to want to give stuff to your children, but giving them too much can create a false sense of entitlement. Children become productive citizens when they work for what they want. Nevertheless, whatever tussles you encounter today with your child, relinquish it to the Master. Give God control of your trouble child while you recapture your strength. He will work your fight into an amazing victory (Romans 8:28). If you were truthful, you would acknowledge that your parents struggled with you at that age too.

I used to think that I was the only parent to deal with child behavioral issues. I am not, and neither are you. The Lord will come to your aid just like He did when the three Hebrew boys who were in a heated dilemma (Daniel 4). Notice, the Lord didn't deliver the Hebrew boys from their fiery furnace; He joined them in their plight. Likewise, He has joined you and your child in your storm and will command your tempest winds to be still.

Parenting is a difficult task. Those lovely, cute, and adorable children take lots of love, energy, and patience. Merge that with life's worries—such as your job, mortgage, bills, and relationships—and it adds up to frustration. You will cry. All parents sob while grooming their children for adulthood. I know I do.

Frustrated Parents

Frustration is defined as unresolved problems that plummet into agitation. In the context of the family, it's the inability to control a situation derived from a power struggle between parent and child. Sometimes it appears the child is winning; it's all in how the parent perceives the war.

I asked a few parents what frustrated them most about their children. This is what they had to share:

- "My son is severely handicapped (that's why I only had one), and as a result, he's never had behavior-type problems, just medical. My biggest frustration is with normal kids. They never appreciate the physical gifts they have. (My late departed co-worker, Frank.)"

- "They don't listen! I can say the same thing until I am blue in the face and *it's in one ear and out the other.* Their need to counterattack everything I say. If I say, "There is a mess in the kitchen," they will say, "No, Mommy, it is only four dishes and three cups." They also bicker daily!"

- "What frustrates me the most about my son is his easy-going nature; he walks like he has all day to get anywhere."

- "What frustrated me was during my divorce, the emotions, anger, and disrespect from the younger two."

- "They are at an age where they know better and act as if they are three."

Can you relate to the statements above? One thing to consider is your approach when dealing with your child's behavior. Your attitude determines your success or failure in handling your child's demeanor. First, step back from your feelings and carefully contemplate what change is needed to maintain a healthy relationship between you and your child. Not all behavior needs addressing. The most common function of behavior is to attain or avoid an uncomfortable situation. Try to pinpoint the source of your child's conduct; it could be emotional, psychological, or physical.

Second, under no circumstance look at yourself as a failure or at your child as unmanageable. Start with your expectations of your child. Determine if those expectations are attainable or not. You shape your child's behavior. For example, if you use inappropriate language around your child, don't be alarmed when your child echoes the same words. Find a plan that diffuses volatile behavior, and get your child to accept responsibility for his actions.

Third, allow your child space to make mistakes; after all, he or she is a child. Your child is going to make more mistakes as he or she gets older, but at the same time, teach your child to learn from his or her mistakes. If your child is of writing age, have him or her write down the mistakes. Review the list often to avoid repeating the same mistakes. Your child needs to know that for every blunder there are repercussions. Although it appears your child is not listening, he or she is. When your child becomes an adult, he or she will thank you for everything you taught him or her—I thank my parents every day.

Moses Frustration with God's Children

There is a story in the Bible for every situation. Moses' story in the book of Exodus screams frustration. God sent Moses to Egypt to get his people from the ruthless dictator, Pharaoh. With God's divine help, Moses persuaded Pharaoh to let the children of Israel go. With much anguish and the death of his son, Pharaoh gladly obliged. The Israelites made their journey across the Red Sea, ate manna and quail from heaven, drank water from a rock, defeated their enemies, received laws to govern their behavior, worshiped, sinned, and were punished for their sins in the desert.

After a long voyage across desert sands, Moses and the Israelites settled in Kadesh. Thereafter, Moses sister died. He grieved the loss of his sister. If that wasn't enough, the Israelites once again complained about the lack of water and dying in the desert, saying, "If only we remained in Egypt, our lives would be better." Stressed, Moses went to God a broken man asking for guidance.

You do the same with your child. You crawl to the altar for guidance and healing. God listened to Moses and didn't react in His usual manner when the Israelites sinned. He calmly told Moses to take his rod, go, *"speak"* to the rock, and give the people water (Numbers 20:7–8). Moses saw no anger in God's tone toward defiant Israel. God's behavior reminds me how grandparents interact with their grandchildren. When you were growing up you couldn't get away with anything, but when your child does something, he gets away with it. You expect your parents to discipline your child, but they don't. Likewise, God didn't handle Moses situation like Moses thought God should have. Similar to Moses, you cry at the feet of the Master to handle your child. You're irrational, unfocused, and out-of-control; whereas, your Father in heaven is very much in control of all things and full of wisdom.

Filled with frustration and anger, Moses went to God's children and said, "Hear now, ye rebels, must we fetch you water out of this rock?" (Numbers 20:10). Must "we" fetch you water? First, God supplied the water. Second, Moses was furious God didn't punish the people nor did He show His anger towards them as He did in times past. James says, "The wrath of man worketh not the righteousness of God" (James 1:20). In other words, anger does not produce the righteous life that God desires. Moses let anger get the best of him, and so do we. We lose control, saying, doing, and planting images that cause dysfunctional families.

Instead of following God's directions, Moses hit the rock. Now God became angry at Moses' disobedience and handed down a severe penalty—not allowing Moses to enter the Promised Land. Moses lost his sister, was the leader of a rebellious nation, and was unable to enter the Promised Land. What a pickle of a situation he got himself into. Despite all Moses endured, his efforts were not in vain (1 Corinthians 15:58). God was still with Moses, just as He is with you. Your child troubles won't last. You will outlive this cumbersome road. Your child will grow up and have a family of his or her own. Then you'll look back over your shoulder at all you struggle with now and smile. You will smile because pay back is coming. Your children's children will give them what they gave you.

Behavior

My twins finally blossomed into their own personalities. In the beginning, they wanted everything alike—toys, clothes, and their circle of friends. I asked God to bring them into their own sense of belonging. I got my wish. Jeremiah, my personality on legs, is a ball of energy. He could run a football field three times and still have the energy of four more children. My struggle with him was to slow him down enough to focus on something, anything. He jumped from project to project. On the other hand, Nehemiah grew into a hellion. My quiet, shy, lovable child was defiant, harmed those who defriended him, and defaced school furniture, and his behavior escalated.

Both my sons are skilled in lying. They would look me in the face without blinking an eye and lie to me. I experienced a roller coaster of emotions that I didn't think was possible. However, I managed to control my anger and frustration by mediating on God's Word, trusting in His promises, and prayer. After speaking with other parents, I discovered I wasn't alone, and neither are you.

You can't control your child's behavior or attitude. Trying to do so will only anger and frustrate you more. Spend your energy on what you can control, like your response to the behavior. Instead of getting irate, look for creative techniques to steer your child away from your child's rebellious deeds. Try to identify what triggers your child's behavior. Delineate between what's acceptable behavior and what's not. You own the key to your child's environment. Sensor what enters your child's mind through television and computers. Control your child's selection of friends. It's your job to correct unacceptable behavior through discipline. Paul writes, "No chastening for the present seemeth to be joyous, but grievous; afterward it yieldeth the peaceable fruit of righteousness unto them which are exercised thereby" (Hebrews 12:11).

Chastisement is not a happy or a joyous occasion. Although it may seem unpleasant, it produces fruits of righteousness. Don't allow your child's behavior to pile up over time; deal with each issue as it transpires. "He that handles a matter wisely shall find good and whoso trusteth in the Lord, happy is he" (Proverbs 16:20). Some children take longer to get the message than others. Be consistent. Stay the course. Never give up. *Where would you be if your parents gave up on you?* You can get through this with prayer. Believe that God answered your prayers (Hebrews 11:6). When your obedient faith is present, the Lord will direct you and your child's footsteps along life's paths in the midst of your difficulties. Remember, your child troubles won't last; you do. Years from now both you and your child will laugh about this, just as you did with your parents. It's just a bump in the road, as with all of life's trials; it doesn't last.

Train Your Child

Proverbs 22:6 says, "Train up a child in the way he should go, and when he gets old, he won't depart from it." It's a biblical command.

To train means to instruct, or to guide. The only way you can instruct or guide your child is by spending time with him (Deuteronomy 6:4-8). The church can only enlighten him about God's love. God is depending on you to teach your own child right and wrong.

If you are one of those parents who drops your child off with friends and relatives every chance you get, stop doing that. You can't direct your child if he or she is not around. Do you not know you are allowing others to mold your child into the person he or she will become in the future? You are selling your child's soul to the devil. Where do you think your child's bad habits come from? Yes, some are from you, but the majority of those bad habits are from the very people they spend most of their time around. What's really scary is you are responsible for those little souls and God is holding you accountable, whether you do or don't do your job as a parent. This could be the very thing that keeps you out of heaven.

Furthermore, let your child live out his life's dreams, not yours. You work overtime at the risk of your own health to send your child to the best schools. Some of you go as far as selecting your child's course curriculum, doing their homework, and picking out the sports he or she will play. You've planned your child's life from cradle to college and sometimes into adulthood. *Are you pushing your child to have a bright future for himself or herself or for you?* When your child refuses to do well in school or is diverted to another career goal, do you become frustrated, upset, and mad? Why?

I was in basic training with a girl who enlisted because her mother forced her. Tammy was a loner and didn't talk much. Not that she couldn't talk; I guess she didn't have a desire to say anything.

Every night I watched her write in her journal. During one of our weekly inspections, our training instructor got in Tammy's face and screamed, then threw her neatly folded T-shirts onto the bathroom floor. He was the verbal straw that broke Tammy. That same night, she attempted to commit suicide. I visited her in the base hospital over the following weeks. The staff chained her down like a wild animal. I asked why she wanted to take her life, and she responded, "I never wanted to be in the military. My mother made me enlist so she could receive my military benefits. I wanted to go to college to become a doctor." I asked her if she had expressed her concerns with her mom. She said, "Yes, over and over, but my mom wouldn't hear of it. My mom would have enlisted in the military herself, but she got pregnant with me, so I owed her."

Wow! That's pressure. If your child's path is a positive and notable one, then let him or her choose his or her own way. It may hurt you that your child didn't join your ole alma mater or wasn't an inductee into the family fraternity, but be thankful that he or she is doing something productive. Be elated your child isn't in jail, or worse—dead.

Regain Your Focus

There's a mental trap that most parents stumble into—a trap that zaps their focus. That trap is child behavior. Raising children takes patience and lots of energy. To survive and thrive, you must keep your eyes on Jesus (Hebrews 12:2). Isaiah 26:4 says, "Thy will keep him in perfect peace, whose mind is stayed on thee; because he trusteth in thee." The passage is saying that if you keep your mind on the Lord, regardless of your circumstances, you will have peace that surpasses all understanding (Philippians 4:7).

A troublesome child can cloud your perspective and make you question God, *Why me?* However, the Bible clears the fog of doubt through its truth in how to train your child. The Bible tells us that God cannot lie (Titus 1:2). By knowing this Bible-based truth, you can confidently be assured that when God says He is your strength during troubled times, He is truly that (Psalm 46:1). You are never alone, especially when you follow His script for raising children. He will stick with you through it all (Proverbs 18:24).

Walk in your circumstance by faith. Everything God is going to do for you has already been done. You access your desires through faith Romans 5:2). Too bad a child handbook wasn't handed to you when your child was born. That would have been greatly appreciated. Since you can't rely on your own methods in raising your child, you need help; get your directives from God's word (Proverbs 3:5–7). While you wait on the Lord, draw your strength from heaven. Isaiah 40:31 says, "They that wait upon the Lord shall renew their strength; they shall mount up with wings as eagles; they shall run, and not be weary; and they shall run, and not lose faith."

There is a happy day coming your way if you faint not (Galatians 6:9). Your storm may take days, months, or even years before you see relief. It's not over until God has the final say. Satan speaks damnation on your child, but God speaks life into your little one (Jeremiah 29:11). There's peace and hope in your conundrums. Keep trusting and holding on until the Lord gives you the green light. When the pressure gets to be too much, take a pause from all distractions around you. Sit quietly in prayer, search the scriptures, fast, and wait. The Comforter will take your petition before God (John 16:13). You cannot rely on your own feelings; however, your faith in Jesus is secure and legitimate.

Noah didn't rely on his own intellect. The scriptures says God told him to build an ark in the middle of a desert and he did it—no questions asked. He didn't know what a boat was and never saw rain. His task was tedious. The ark took 120 years to build. He didn't complain. He trusted God with all his heart, soul, and mind. Even when God told him to gather two of every kind of animal and bring them into the ark, Noah didn't ask how to accomplish such a task. *Can you imagine Noah chasing a squirrel into the ark, then going out to get a mate for him?* My point is Noah obeyed God, and so should you. We treat God as if He is human. We dictate our wants at Him rather than kneel before His grace. The lessons learned from Noah are these:

1. Plan ahead.
2. Keep praying
3. Stop what you are doing and do what God says! Those little ones need you.

If you do not remember anything I've written, remember that with God all things are possible (Luke 1:37) and there nothing too hard for Him (Genesis 18:14). You may raise your child, but God decides the direction your child goes (Proverbs 16:9). He has your child etched in the palms of His almighty hands (Isaiah 49:16). He knows your child's end before he or she began.

Being a Christian doesn't mean you won't experience sadness, loneliness, or seasons of hardships. It means you won't experience these things alone. David said, "Yea, though I walk through the valley of the shadow of death, I will fear no evil for thou art with me" (Psalm 23:4). You shouldn't worry or fret over your child's behavior. It won't last because your child won't be young forever. Enjoy your time with him or her while you can.

Working and Unappreciated

*Experience is what you get when you didn't get
what you wanted.*
—Unknown

Another bad day at work? Don't be startled or filled with anxiety. It's just a day. As the old spiritual song goes, "This earth is not my home, I'm just passing through." Put the computer down and breathe. Throwing it against the wall isn't a good way to deal with work-related stress. If you find yourself having more bad days than good ones and feeling unappreciated, you have a stronghold problem. The apostle Paul writes:

> For though we walk in the flesh, we don't war after the flesh, for the weapons of our warfare are not carnal, but mighty through God to the pulling down of strongholds, casting down imagination and every high thing that exalts itself against the knowledge of God, and bring into captivity every thought to the obedience of Christ (2 Corinthians 10:3–5).

In other words, the annoyed feelings you sense toward your workplace and the people are tricks of devil (2 Corinthians 2:11). He has you feeling frustrated, unappreciated, and defeated. He wants you to walk away from your job and make you think you'll find another job—as if this economy is going to hand another job to you without the normal job search woes. Don't listen to Satan. He will destroy all you worked hard for; just ask Adam and Eve. Satan convinced the first couple to partake of the very tree God warned them not to eat of (Genesis 3:1). Rather than being thankful for the trees they could eat of, their attention was drawn to what they couldn't have. Don't concentrate on the negative aspects of your job. Instead, praise God you have a job.

Look at it this way: you don't work for your boss; you work for God. The Bible says, "Whatsoever ye do, do it heartily, as to the Lord, and not unto men" (Colossian 3:23). Worrying over injustice done against you will only make you angrier and hinder you from being, as Paul describes, "a written epistle" in your workplace. Your life is an open book to your coworkers and bosses. They are witnesses of your words and actions (2 Corinthians 3:2). God sent you there to lead someone to Christ, just as He sent Phillip to the Ethiopian eunuch in Acts 8. You were not given your job to pay bills; God already said He will take care of your needs (Philippians 4:19).

You are a CIA agent for God, an undercover Christian in action. You're the mole in the organization sent to combat organized sin through prayer and fasting (Ephesians 6:18). Rejoice! God is going to bring about a change in your hour of despair. Pray immediately when worry enters your mind (Romans 12:12). God will send his ministering angels to your location (Hebrews 1:14).

The atrocity you endure in your workplace won't last. You will outlive this ordeal. The psalmist David writes, "Wait on the Lord, be of good courage, and He shall strengthen thine heart, wait I say, on the Lord" (Psalm 27:14). Therefore, whatever your boss asks you to do, whether in a wicked tone, a malicious spirit, or a retaliatory manner, do it to the glory of God (1 Corinthians 10:31), as long as it doesn't violate God's word. Let God handle the rest. Forgiveness relieves tension and stress, so forgive those who trouble you as many times as needed (Matthew 18:21). You are there to show the love of Christ. This is a hard task, but someone has to do it. Don't worry, the Holy Spirit gave you everything you need to perform your job (1 Corinthians 12:11). Besides, God's job benefits outweigh any benefits you are currently getting from your current employer. Job troubles don't last, you do!

Bad Days

You may leave the house feeling like you're on top of the world, and by noon the world is on top of you. Persecution awaits everyone who tries to live godly according to 2 Timothy 3:12. Deadlines have stressed you to the point of overeating. Office friction places you in an awkward position because you won't choose sides. Then the sides band together against you. Now your phenomenal work is considered substandard because you refuse to be a team player in interoffice politics. Your days are bad and numbered.

I'll let you in on a secret: neither your supervisor nor your coworkers have power over you. You didn't get your job because of your resume or because a buddy of yours recommended you. God strategically placed you at your place of employment. You're in the middle of a war between good and evil. As a Christian, this is not news to you. You already know how the story ends according to the book of Revelation. The war was won through Christ's death (Colossians 2:14). It's time you live like the fight was won.

It's not easy watching those around you who do the minimum work and get the recognition. In fact, it's frustrating and hurtful. Nonetheless, remember who owns you. Galatians 6:4 tells us to, "let every man prove his own work, and then shall he have rejoicing in himself alone, and not in others." In other words, don't compare what you do with what others do. Do your best. God won't forget you (1 Corinthians 15:58). When you keep your eyes on Him, you will find perfect peace (Isaiah 26:3).

The apostle Paul faced trials one after another with no sign of relief. He had many bad days. When Paul departed for Jerusalem, the Holy Spirit warned him that prison and hardship awaited him there. By faith Paul traveled to Jerusalem anyway. Likewise, you may not know what devious plot your supervisor has in store to thwart your efforts, but go to work anyway. Trust Jesus to clear the landmines of your office battlefield before you arrive. He will step into your storm and calm your raging sea. He is your very-present help (Psalm 46:1). Imitate Paul's "let none of these things move me" attitude (Acts 20:24). Don't just hear God's will but do it. Position yourself as a strong tree. Life storms will blow. However, with your spiritual tree roots buried deeper beyond the soil, you won't fall (Matthew 7:22–27). If God is for you, who can be against you (Romans 8:31)? Besides, who shall separate you from the love of Christ? "Shall tribulation, or distress, or persecution or famine, or nakedness, or peril or sword?" Paul was persuaded that neither death, nor life (your job, your boss, and your coworkers), nor angels, nor principalities, nor powers, nor things present, nor things to come, nor height, nor depth, nor any other creature, shall be able to separate you from the love of God, which is in Christ Jesus our Lord (Romans 8:35–39).

Paul didn't say what shall keep Christ from loving you, but I ask the question: *What will keep you from loving the Savior?* Tragedy may affect your devotion to Jesus, but it won't cause Jesus to leave or forsake you. You're safely tucked under His loving shelter of omnipresence and omnipotence. Satan has no domination over you. The only power he has is what you give him. For instance, if you had a home invasion and the burglar didn't have a gun and your gun was loaded, wouldn't that change your home invasion scenario? Likewise, Jesus's resurrection rendered Satan powerless, granting you help from heaven and the power to ignore everything Satan says. Therefore, your job troubles are only temporary. They won't last, you do.

God behind the Scene

The norm seems to motivate slackers with bonuses and praise, while hard-working employees get more work. It may appear the unrighteous are winning, but "Be ye steadfast, unmovable, always abounding in the work of the Lord, forasmuch as you know that your labor is not in vain" (1 Corinthians 15:58). You missed that last part: "your labor is *not* in vain." When you don't think you can't go on, God empowers you to keep going. Yes, you deserve a bigger raise. Yes, your boss is getting credit for your ideas. Yes, you deserve the recognition for the enormous project you labored months on that was a success.

God offers spiritual and emotional healing. Don't get discouraged; you will be rewarded for your work. Know that suffering produces "patience, and patience experience [character], and experience hope: and hope makes not ashamed because the love of God is shed abroad in our hearts by the Holy Spirit, which was given unto us" (Romans 5:3–5). If God brought you to your place of employment, He'll bring you through, whatever befalls you! Don't let the devil steal your joy.

My beloved, you have special privileges in your arsenal according to Ephesians 1:3. One privilege of being a child of God is twenty-four-hour access to the Father. You need no appointment. Paul writes, "Be careful for nothing; but in everything by prayer and supplication with thanksgiving let your request be made known unto God" (Philippians 4:6). God will sustain you through your prayers (Psalm 55:22). Don't allow Satan to talk you out of your job like he talked Adam and Eve out of their home. Their home was a gift just as your job is a gift from God. The Father gives good gifts. Instead of complaining, give thanks. Praise moves God to act on your behalf. Your injustice won't last. God knows what He is doing. He allows Satan's attack without interference because He has a plan.

What is done against you in your workplace, God will bring about a good from it just as He did for Joseph. Joseph went from the pit of depression to the palace of reform. He went from slavery to being a ruler; God will do the same for you (Genesis 50:20). All things work together for the good of those who love God and are called according to His purpose (Romans 8:38).

The prophet Habakkuk faced a similar situation during his lifetime. It wasn't in a work setting, but the lesson is applicable. Habakkuk wrestled with injustice during his time. He questioned why God allowed evil people to go unpunished and let the righteous suffer. The answer to Habakkuk's question was startling. God told Habakkuk not to worry. He would repay Israel for their sins by raising up a nation of ruthless people, the Babylonians, to chastise them. Whatever is happening in your workplace that is unfair and unjust, take it to the Master. He will remove the one that troubles you or elevate someone who will bring strife and hardship to the one that causes you grief. Just sit back and wait. All you can do is, "If it be possible, as much as lieth in you, live peaceably with all men" (Romans 12:18). God is behind the scenes working miracles in your life right now. Whatever God speaks into existence; it happens— review creation in Genesis 1. Your inequality will be dealt with because God knows how to bring about vengeance (Romans 12:19).

The Enemy

Jesus teaches His disciples that a person's conduct reveals his true character: "the tree is known by his fruit" (Matthew 12:33). Satan can't use bodies that are full of light. He uses coworkers, bosses, and subordinates to move you from your firm foundation of faith by infiltrating bodies that are already filled with darkness to do his dirty deeds against you. Then you react and lose the fight. God's creation teaches a lesson about good and evil. Light and darkness cannot occupy the same space. Jesus said, "Every good tree bringeth forth good fruit; but a corrupt tree bringeth forth evil fruit. A good tree cannot bring forth evil fruit; neither can a corrupt tree bring forth good fruit" (Matthew 7:17–19). Your true enemy is Satan.

You may feel that your enemies are your co-workers and bosses, but in reality, their bodies have been invaded by Satan. There's a spiritual warfare taking place in the spiritual realm that's manifesting itself in your physical realm. You feel the effects, but you are not physically seeing the war. When your job seems unbearable and the walls are caving in around you, put on your spiritual armor (Ephesians 6:11–17). This war can't be fought with what you see; it takes a special kind of uniform, one that will slice and dice in the spiritual world. According to Ephesians 6:10, faith is one of those garments that needs donning. Be on your guard for your boss's evil squint, hostile comments, documentation, and counseling sessions. These are used to disrupt your success. Stand firm in your faith and be strong (1 Corinthian 16:13). You are not going anywhere until the Lord says so.

Did you not know that your enemies are self-esteem and confidence builders? You have something your enemies wished they had. They don't know it, but that something is Christ. Coworkers and bosses lash out when they're experiencing rejection and inadequacy. The root cause is envy. Proverbs 3:31 says, "Envy rottens the bones." It reaches the very core of a person's true intent. However, none of their office tactics will keep you from what God has in store for you. If you react to your office drama in a scriptural fashion, you will win every time. Here are a few scriptures to mediate upon during office trials:

> Do not be overcome by evil, but overcome evil with good (Romans 12:21).

> But I say unto you which hear, love your enemies, do good to them which hate you. Bless them that curse you, and pray for them which despitefully use you (Luke 6:27–28).

> No weapon that is formed against me shall prosper; and every tongue that shall rise against thee in judgment thou shalt condemn. This is the heritage of the servants of the Lord, and their righteousness is of me, saith the Lord (Isaiah 54:17).

> But he that doeth wrong shall receive for the wrong which he hath done; and there is no respect of person (Colossians 3:21).

> As ye know how we exhorted and comforted and charged every one of you, as a father doeth his children, that you would walk worthy of God, who hath called you unto his kingdom and glory (1 Thessalonians 2:11–12).

> Seeing it a righteous thing with God to recompense [repay] tribulation to them that trouble you (2 Thessalonians 1:6).

Conflict Resolution

Conflict in itself is normal and healthy in relationships. Everyone is different in their thinking and perspectives. This makes each of us unique. We can't agree on everything all the time. However, agreeing to disagree can be challenging at times too. Paul makes it clear that each Christian has different spiritual gifts. When those gifts are combined, God's work is accomplished (1 Corinthians 12). When we work with those who are not easy to work with, two things will happen: 1) God's manifestation is revealed in the workplace; and 2) a change takes place in the hearts of the evildoers. In order to accomplish both tasks, you will have to remain calm and in control of your emotions and respect other people's differences. It's not easy to maintain a level head in the midst of office drama, but it's essential. Expect trials. God allowing your trials helps you:

- See others' true nature. When you know what you are dealing with, you will know how to pray (Luke 1:71).

- See your own nature. Repent and refocus your thoughts on the Lord. Walk in the light as He is in the light (1 John 1:7).

- Understand and endure trials now. You will enjoy heavenly bliss later.

- Surrender your will to God's will. Trust Him to handle the details of your life.

Conflict resolution is obtainable when you know the mediator (1 Timothy 2:5). Defer your fight to Jesus. Give the steering wheel to Him, and let Him drive. Take your rest in the backseat. The battle belongs to the Lord anyway! The winner of this race is not the one who moves fast through this life, and neither is it to the strong, intelligent, rich, or powerful; it's the one who endures trials and temptations (Ecclesiastes 9:11). Christians resolve conflicts by praying, living soberly, righteously, and godly in this present world (Titus 2:10). You have everything you need to overcome your office conflict. It is time to apply God's Word in your life. You will be amazed at the outcome. Have faith!

Job asked his wife a valid question during his ordeal: "What? Shall we receive good at the hand of God and not receive evil?" The Bible says Job didn't sin by making that statement. You will experience injustices and trials in this life, and God will allow Satan to have his way with you, but Satan can only go as far as God allows (Job 2:1-10). You will do good to remember who the Father is and the power He holds. Your troubles won't last. You will overcome your workplace opposition. If anything, God may move your enemies and let you remain in your workplace. It has happened to many of you already. Continue to stay prayed up.

Money Woes

Greed is not a financial issue. It's a heart issue
—Andy Stanley

Financial concerns weighing you down? Is your debt inducing stress and anxiety? Do you fear losing material possessions due to an inability to pay your bills? Your apprehension is the result of Satan's spiritual captivity. According to 2 Timothy 1:7, God didn't give you the spirit of fear but power to vanquish your debt and the ability to raise your credit score. The clincher between success and failure in your financial matters is self-control. Discipline is the attribute that gives victory over your iniquitous desire.

Besiege your economic future through prayer and financial planning. Your money atrocities don't only impact you; they affect the Lord's church and its growth. If you refuse to control your spending for heavenly reasons, then sanction it for your children. Don't bequeath debt; bequest a legacy of godly righteousness. Simply put, curb your impulses. Thomas Jefferson said, "Nothing can stop the man with the right mental attitude from achieving his goal; nothing on earth can help the man with the wrong mental attitude."

Although you may be in the middle of a financial crisis right now, take a stand against impulse spending. As a solider of the Lord, you don't run from hardship; you take a stand and fight. Put on your godly armor and keep it on (Ephesians 6:11). Your money battles hinge heavily on what battle attire you wear. When Satan whispers in your ear that you can't win against bad debt and makes it difficult for you to save money, the Bible says, "Take up the shield of faith" (Ephesians 6:16). This armor helps you to withstand the evil day. Your evil day is when nothing goes right in your life, such as the need for constant repairs on your car or burst pipes in the home. You go from one atrocity to the next with no relief in sight. Satan is trying to ruin you. But God is so amazing. How awesome is God? He will guide you through your maze of financial commitments and take care of your needs. Lay aside your financial weight. Run your financial race with patience (Hebrews 12:2). It is going to take patience to work your way out of debt.

The enemy attacked you though your singleness, your marriage, you children, and your job, and you're still standing! Now, he wants to a take you down through your finances. Stay strong, and witness God's amazing rescue in your life (Job 1:6–8). No matter how frustrated, anxious, and desperate your situation gets, you need to know there's hope in Jesus. He is your strong tower.

> The name of the Lord is a strong tower: the righteous runneth into it and is safe (Proverbs 18:10).

Regretfully, this is not a financial self-help chapter to get you out of the rat race of debt and help you achieve the wealth you seek. This chapter is written to encourage you to hold on to the power within you so you can get through your currency problems. You're a child of the Most High; you will outlive whatever Satan launches at you. Don't obsess over money matters. This can rob you of your heavenly future and keep you from preparing for the Lord's return. Press toward your debt-free goal through prayer and leaning on the Lord (Philippians 3:14).

Jesus paid your debt on the cross. Why are you paying any debt in this life? So stop creating debt! He called you to peace, not debt. Repent and become a better steward of your funds. Don't have misguided expectations of saving hundreds of dollars by robbing God either (Malachi 3:8). God condemned a whole nation, suggesting that robbery was a widespread abuse of His generosity. No one enjoys adversity and pain, but if you neglect to give to God what is His, God will create a situation where you will lose the money you took from Him. You may have already learned this lesson. If not heed the warning.

Your spending addiction is not an ambush; you've had a history of financial issues for a long time. Yet, God keeps delivering you each time (Genesis 22:13–14). It's time to rectify your predicament and adhere to God's Word. You've tried it your way. See where that has gotten you? Put your money matters into God's hands. This chapter speaks to me. I remember this past Christmas, I badly wanted the latest Microsoft Surface, but I didn't have the money to buy it. I allowed Satan to infiltrate my mind with images of owning the device. After work, I went to the electronic store, found the product, and placed it on the counter. Next, I handed the storeowner my visa card. The smile on my face was priceless. The storeowner swiped the card in the card reader and then said, "You were declined." I lost my priceless smile. I was embarrassed, upset, and ashamed. The ten people behind me pretended they didn't hear the conversation. Thankfully, the card reader didn't spit the card out while saying, "Put that thing back in your purse. You're broke." I had reached my credit limit, and the repercussions were debt, no savings, and bad credit.

I had debt as if I owned a business. I have to say advertisers do an excellent job in marketing their products. Their luring technique is similar to that of Satan where he deceives through bargains, which turns out to be entrapment. I was enticed into accepting credit cards with low interest rates for the first year. The following year, I couldn't financially keep up with my obligations. Now I know there's a guaranteed way to get everything you want: want less.

Don't be destroyed by greed. Anything above what you can afford is greed. It's time to repent. Repent is a military term to do an about face. It's a 180-degree turn from where you stand. That should position you in the opposite direction. Stop living a life of unbelief. Didn't God say He would take care of you? He will supply all your needs (Philippians 4:19). You may think you need more, but God has given you what you can handle.

The very thing that you struggle with most brings you closer to Jesus (Psalm 34:18). Jonah learned this lesson in the belly of a whale. The disciples learned this lesson in the midst of the sea (Mark 6:47-48). The three Hebrew boys learned this lesson in a fiery furnace. God gives peace for despair. Don't let your money matters move you from your position of faith in Jesus (Acts 20:24). Keep trusting. Keep holding on. Reach for the sky. As long as you give yourself to Christ, you can have what you want if you keep pressing on. Your payday is around the corner. Here are a few entries to add to your financial checklist:

1. Thank God for what you have. Just think, you could lose it in a fire, a thief could break in and steal it, or a violent storm could destroy it.

2. Remove all your credit cards from your wallet. Take only the cash you need for the occasion.

3. Map out your destination, and go only to the places you need to go. Then return home.

4. Stop hanging out with friends who spend money. Tell them you are on a budget. Unless they sympathize with your condition and pay your way, avoid them.

5. Don't use ATMs that are not in your banking network. Save those fees.

6. Envision your goal. See yourself with the wealth you always wanted. Keep your eyes on the prize (Philippians 3:14).

7. Ask God to curb your spending habit. This doesn't mean to ask Him for help, then continue your uncontrollable spending practices. Fall on your knees and find rest in Him (Psalm 62:1).

8. Put aside monies for God, then put away some for a rainy day. Watch God work.

The key to a financial stress-free life is a heart fixed on God's word:

> The Lord is good to those who wait for him, to the soul who seeks him (Lamentations 3:25).

> Wait for the Lord; be strong, and let your heart take courage; wait for the Lord (Psalm 27:14)!

> And now, O Lord, for what do I wait? My hope is in you (Psalm 39:7).

> But they who wait for the Lord shall renew their strength; they shall mount up with wings like eagles; they shall run and not be weary; they shall walk and not faint (Isaiah 40:31).

> For God alone, O my soul, wait in silence, for my hope is from him (Psalm 62:5).

> I can do all things through Christ which strengthens me (Philippians 4:13).

> The blessing of the Lord, it make rich and he added no sorrow with it (Proverbs 10:22).

When you are in life's trenches because of your own doing, Jesus will get in your downward spiral with you, understand your plight, and bring you out of your hopeless situation. In Psalm 23, David started out talking *about* God, but by verse 4, he began talking *to* God:

> The Lord is my shepherd; I shall not want. He maketh me to lie down in green pastures: he leadeth me

beside the still waters. He restoreth my soul: he leadeth me in the paths of righteousness for his name's sake. Yea, though I walk through the valley of the shadow of death, I will fear no evil: for thou art with me, thy rod and thy staff they comfort me.

Although your financial storm appears dim, it's known throughout the book of Revelation that you're destined to succeed. David said he had not seen the righteous forsaken nor his seed begging bread (Psalm 37:25). Stop complaining, and thank God for what you have right now, even if there's nothing in your pocket. A thank-you goes a long way with God. He will exceed your expectations (Ephesians 3:20–21).

Pocket with Holes

It was a hot summer's day, and I had lost my earrings. I thought I had put them in my pants pocket, but they weren't there. I looked everywhere for them, on counters and tables, even the pockets of my clothing in the closet. Not finding them, I continued to flip over pillows and run my fingers along the floorboards. Eventually, I became exhausted and gave up. Then I decided to search my pants pockets once more. To my surmise, I found holes in my pockets!

There is one thing the Old Testament has plenty of, and that is life-changing stories. One story in particular reminded me of bags with holes in them (Haggai 1:1–18). God saw His people living in their nice homes and His house was in shambles. The people put their own comfort before finishing the house of God. Upset and disappointed, God told Haggai, the prophet, to tell the people to "consider their ways," that their hard work would be in vain. They would eat and not get full, have clothes and not get warm, make money but see no profit—like putting it in a bag with holes, they would lose it as fast as they made it. They had no desire to please the one who blessed them. Therefore, God lost the zeal to continue to bless the people. God sent a message by Haggai that all their efforts would be a waste of time. Agricultural and economic disaster resulted from God's withdrawal because the people failed to please Him.

Don't be like Israel. Honor God with your first fruits. God asks you to trust Him with all you own and He will pour out blessings from heaven you cannot contain (Malachi 3:10). You owe everything to the one who for your sake "made himself nothing" (Philippians 2:7; 2 Corinthians 8:9). Break the bad spending habits that broke your monthly budget before it's too late. Did you not know that God takes great delight in His creation and rejoices over it with singing (Zephaniah 3:17)? But sometimes His creation makes Him cry because He is placed last on its list. Prioritize your goals. Don't continue your path or God will line your pockets with holes. Seek Him first in all things.

Sounds Like a Good Idea

In the minds of men, Satan does his best work. He plays out vivid imagery in the human mind and choreographs storylines that lead us to our demise. Judas thought it was a good idea to betray the Son of God for thirty pieces of silver. Like all ideas, it sounded good in his head, until it was acted out. Judas' greed plunged him into destruction (1 Timothy 6:10). No one forced him to betray Jesus, not even the devil. The devil merely created the scenario for Judas to hand Jesus over to the chief priests to be murdered. In return, the chief priests rewarded Judas with thirty pieces of silver. Nevertheless, this transaction didn't catch Jesus by surprise. Jesus told the apostles of his betrayal, then exposed His betrayer to the group saying, "Truly, I say to you, one of you will betray me" (Matthew 26:21). The rumble echoed throughout the upper room, "Is it I?" Jesus ended the chatter by saying, "It is he to whom I shall give this morsel when I have dipped it." Judas was the recipient of the dipped bread. He should have walked away from the chief priests' offer.

There's something about the love of money that makes a person do the unthinkable. We aren't told about Judas' profession as we are the other apostles, but we are told of his love for money and that he was the keeper of the apostles' money, which was kept in a bag (John 13:29). Judas' money greed flowed into an anger management problem (1 Timothy 6:10). Judas showed his monetary outrage at Lazarus' dinner party in front of the guest of honor, Jesus. While the men sat at the table, Mary anointed Jesus' feet with very expensive oil. After she poured the oil on His feet and dried his feet with her hair, Judas yelled, "The perfume could have been sold and the money given to the poor" (Matthew 26:9). He actually wanted the money for himself. He wasn't only greedy; he was a thief (John 12:4-6).

Sometime later, Judas carried out the betrayal with a kiss; Jesus was arrested and led away. Judas repented and tried to do the right thing by giving back the money to the chief priests, but they wouldn't take it back, so Judas hanged himself (Matthew 27:3–5). What a tragedy over money. It left him with so much guilt and misery, knowing that he had betrayed the very Son of God.

I'm not sure what Judas thought would happen to Jesus, perhaps an interrogation, then business as usual. Nevertheless, Judas was seized with remorse. Don't let money matters trap you into remorse and ungodliness. Satan has a way of taking you farther than you want to go, keeping you longer than you intend to stay, and leaving you with severe consequences. Then, he laughs at your calamity. He even taunts you by saying he didn't make you do it. He is correct! You were tempted and drawn by your own evil desires (James 1:14).

A day is coming when repentance will be too late. Seek the Lord now while He can be found (Isaiah 55:6). When a problematic situation arises, your immediate reaction is to find a solution instead of seeking the Lord first. Discouraged by your own inadequacy in handling the problem, you say all is hopeless. I stop by to tell you to rest in God's sufficiency. Don't ignore the power within you.

Nest Egg

Now's the time to set aside a few extra dollars in preparation for unexpected emergencies. Stop making excuses for not saving money. Put away your credit cards. The rule of thumb should be if you don't have the money for what you want, then don't buy it, a lesson I learned the hard way. Discipline is necessary to accomplish such a feat, and you can only achieve this only through God's strength

(Philippians 4:13). Begin your journey in saving money by seeking God first. You live in the age where online searching is possible to find anything. Why not Google the Bible and find lessons to apply to your financial life? For example, turn to 2 Chronicles 20:3, in which Jehoshaphat tells the people to fast, seek forgiveness of their sins, and ask God for help when he learned that his enemy was coming to defeat him. The lesson to be learned from this story is to apply prayer when you begin your voyage to managing your finances. Start on your knees, giving yourself to the Lord and asking forgiveness for mishandling your funds (Romans 12:2). Second, ask God to help you set aside savings. In verses 5–12, Jehoshaphat prayed. His prayer revealed a few things to apply in your life:

(1) Jehoshaphat committed the situation to God. How often when you run out of money do you hand the matter over to God? He is the only one who can provide the help you need.

(2) Jehoshaphat was a servant of God who sought after God. In the same manner, you are a child of God. Seek God in prayer for deliverance and discernment.

(3) Jehoshaphat praised God's glory and stood on His promises. Did you know there are thirty-five hundred promises in the Bible? When financial dilemmas arise in your life, do you stand on God's promises? Below are a few of those promises. Whenever you see the words "I will," "you will," or "it will," the passage reveals God's promise to you.

Come unto me all ye that labour and are heavy laden, and I will give you rest (Matthew 11:28).

Ask, and it will be given to you; seek and you will find; knock, and it will be opened to you (Luke 11:9).

Whatever you ask in prayer, believe that you have received it, and it will be yours (Luke 11:23).

(4) Jehoshaphat depended solely upon God for deliverance. When it looks like there's no way out, and all hope is lost, remember God is in control. He may change your position (i.e., getting you that house, job, or car you want), but keep you in your condition (i.e., low on funds) until He is ready to change your condition problem to meet your position. God's timing is always on time.

We are told that Jehoshaphat's enemy bore down on him and the people, but God told them to not be afraid for the battle was not theirs, but His. You may not be fighting an enemy army, but every day you battle money temptations and pressures. As a child of God, your financial troubles won't last because you belong to the one who holds the world in His hand. He has your back. Recognize your finiteness, and allow God to work through your fears, weaknesses, and money challenges. He is able to make all grace abound toward you, that you will always have sufficiency in all things, that you may abound in every good work (2 Corinthians 9:8).

Financial Patience

The two hardest tests on your spiritual road are the patience to wait and the courage not to be disappointed while waiting. You may get e-mails or text messages expeditiously; however, saving money takes time. The art of saving is not a sprint; it's a marathon, slow, and one dollar at a time. You obtain financial patience through attitude and determination. You can do it! You are more than a conqueror in Christ Jesus (Romans 8:37). Just put off your old self and forsake the behavior that landed you in your financial predicament. Become a good steward with your monies. Account for every penny you spend by writing down everything you purchase. By doing so, you will learn something about your spending habits.

Put away a few dollars each pay period. If you stick with it, you will reap big dividends. Start today. Don't put off what you can do now. However, there is one thing you can put off, and that is your old man (Ephesians 4:22). Discard your previous money management lifestyle. It wasn't working for you anyway. Start your savings in Jesus's strength, not your own ingenuity. You are nothing without the one who created you.

Of course, Satan won't be happy with your new way of life and will plant an impatient seed in your mind. Ignore him. He has no power over you. Jesus stepped on his head coming out of the grave, disabling him and making him powerless (Genesis 3:15).

Satan was crafty in getting Eve to want more than God had given, and he uses that same tactic today. There is a lesson in the Bible for every mortal situation. In Genesis 3:1–6, Satan started his sneaky attack by asking Eve a simple question, "Did God actually

71

say you shall not eat of any tree in the garden?" He knew what God told them to do and not to do; he was there. He tested Eve's knowledge. Then he added, "For God knows that when you eat of it your eyes will be opened and you will be like God, knowing good and evil." Since Satan knew the rules of the game, he got her to desire the dangling fruit. He is doing the same with you when you spend monies that you don't have by using credit cards.

You've been tricked into switching over to Satan's disillusion side instead of remaining on God's truth-based side. The truth is you have no money. Satan makes you think you will charge a small amount and when you are paid, you will pay it off. Not so. You end up robbing Peter to pay Paul, an old expression referring to the bad habit of shuffling your money to pay bills. Then you have no money and revert to credit cards once again.

Walk in the light as God is in the light, and God will deliver you from your bondage of debt (1 John 1:7). Listen to the Holy Spirit, who will guide you into all truth (John 16:13). He uses positive convictions to warn you against unhealthy financial behavior and lovingly nudges you back to the Lord. Don't let Satan play with your mind. Ground yourself in the Scriptures. You will make it through your financial troubles, I promise. You are a child of God. Your financial troubles won't last, you do.

Death

*I'm not afraid of death; I just don't want to be there
when it happens.*
—Woody Allen

Death is a subject no one wants to confer, consider, or consult on. The topic never comes up in a casual conversation. Even if you alluded to it, friends and family would have you institutionalized. However, maybe we *should* discuss our death plans. After all, a sundry of people are parading through life like there's no eternity. How is it that we can plan life events such as weddings and vacations, but not our own mortality? The time to pre-plan your afterlife is now. This is not paranoia talking, it's reality.

Everyone wants to go to heaven, but no one wants to die; however, death is unavoidable (Romans 5:11). "What man is he that liveth and shall not see death?" (Psalm 89:48). Enoch (Genesis 5:24) and Elijah (2 Kings 2:11) are the only men I've read about that evaded death according to the scriptures. Since such recording, I've not heard of any other. One thing I know about death is that it will come like a thief in the night (Luke 12:13-21). A thief doesn't leave a note nor make noise during a home invasion; he visits when you least expect him. Similarly, Jesus will return when we least expect

Him. Death isn't a secret; the Word of God tells us what we can expect when we die.

> And the graves were opened; and many bodies of the saints which slept arose (Matthew 27:52).

> For David, after he had served his own generation by the will of God, fell asleep, and was laid unto his fathers, and saw corruption (Acts 13:36). The phrase "saw corruption" means his body decayed.

> We shall not all sleep, but we shall all be changed, in a moment, in the twinkling of an eye, at the last trump: for the trumpet shall sound and the dead shall be raised incorruptible and we shall be changed (1 Corinthians 15:51).

Preparing for your death doesn't make you weird or suicidal; it makes you wise (Proverb 12:28). I contemplated how I would like to die, not that I was going to take my life. I elect, if it happened, to go quickly and without pain. Who wouldn't want a painless death? After evaluating my statement, I revise my statement by saying when that time comes, I hope to have time to repent before my expedited departure. Gliding quickly into eternity without preparation isn't good: (1) you won't have time to repent, and (2) you won't have time to say good-bye to your loved ones.

Another thing I can say about death is that it is truly the great equalizer. It is no respecter of person (Romans 2:11). You can't bribe it or talk your way out of it. Regardless of culture, race, sex, finances, and religion, everyone will die (Romans 5:11). It's not up for discussion; your time to die is set. The Hebrew writer pens, "It is appointed unto men once to die, but after this the judgment" (Hebrews 9:27).

When death occurs, it leaves an empty void, a gaping hole in the heart. The psalmist describes such hurt as, "I'm weary with my groaning; all the night I make my bed to swim; I water my couch with my tears" (Psalm 6:6–7). We all feel like this when someone close to us dies. Whether it was a friend, sibling, pet, or even someone you scarcely knew, somehow, death affects us all. You behave in such a way that others notice. It's a helpless situation wherein you can't eat, sleep, or feel hopeful. You feel like you're coming apart. No one can comfort you. You can't believe it happened. Denial and numbness lodge their hooks into your psyche. You become angry and have unexplained emotions. Next, you're depressed.

Nevertheless, don't worry; you will survive. Your outlook will get better. Lean on your sisters and brothers in the Lord for support. If you don't open up to them and acknowledge your hurt, how can they encourage you? If you are the one doing the encouraging, don't share your death stories. Be a listening support. Listening helps the healing process. Take each day as it comes. And remember time heals all wounds. Accept the hurt. It's okay; you are not alone. Take all the time you need to grieve. There's no predictable schedule for grief, and it shouldn't be rushed. God can mend a broken heart, but He must have all the pieces.

This poem I wrote sums it up:

Live Today

Live today; it's a gift.

Tomorrow is like a ship adrift.

Reflect not on tomorrow, it's time borrowed,

For today is sufficient with all its sorrows.

Don't worry about the future or fret things to come.

God has a plan for everyone.

Live your life without regret.

Your hope today Jesus has met.

Trials come and go.

Life continues an even flow.

Then comes the threshing floor.

Judgement begins, and life is no more.

For everything has a season, time will tell,

Living for today in God's holding cell.

Dreams do come true.

Just wait, in heaven we'll live in yonder blue.

Somewhere I heard, "The fear of death follows from the fear of life. A man who lives fully is prepared to die at any time." I say anyone who is faithful to Christ is ready to die. Believers, be at peace with death because Jesus is your anchor. Lift your head and keep holding on. You'll soon see the Son! Your crying will eventually cease (Revelation 21:4). The ache in your heart will disappear. Jesus guarantees His people will reunite with Him in the end. It's the beginning of a journey toward a new and everlasting life. Like everything else, death won't last either; Christians do. You will live on into eternity.

Here Today, Gone Today

A few years ago, a man was absorbed into a sinkhole while asleep in bed. On another occasion, a former and disgruntled TV station employee in Virginia killed a reporter and her camera operator while live on air. In Charleston, North Carolina, nine churchgoers were killed during a Bible study. These deaths were unforeseen. I read a quote somewhere that said, "You may tie your shoes in the morning, you don't know who will untie them at night." No one knows what tomorrow will bring. Death happens so fast that James describes life as a vapor (James 4:14). It's here today and gone today.

Worrying when or how you will die is irrelevant. Don't entertain such thoughts. Paul tells us to avoid questions that are unprofitable and vain (Titus 3:9). You may think it's a fair question to ask, but a more adequate question is: *What do you need to do to prepare for your demise?*

As a child of God, you should be familiar with death and it's concept; it's not a new phenomenon. You read about it in the Bible and have witnessed it during your lifetime, whether among your immediately family and friends or from the nightly news. Death is a recurring event. I encourage you to live each day with Christ. Better yet, live as if it's your last day. You can only blame yourself if you don't make it to heaven; your destiny is in your hands (Matthew 7:13–14).

You may tell yourself you're no murderer, you're kind to everyone, you feed the homeless, and you are hospitable to your neighbors, and that's all you need to be. This is a great error if your life isn't in Christ. Having a life in Christ means being crucified with the Savior to a point that you no longer live for yourself but allow Christ to live in you (Galatians 2:20). You allow the Holy Spirit to lead you in your walk, faith, and love. Calling on the name of the Lord alone doesn't guarantee you a place in heaven. Only those that obey God's commands will make it to that peaceful shore (Matthew 7:21).

Being a good person doesn't secure you a place in heaven either. There's a man in the Bible by the name of Cornelius. He was a good man, upright, God-fearing, and prayed to God all the time. God sent Peter to instruct Cornelius in what he needed to do to obtain the anchor in his life. If Cornelius was a good man alone, why did God send Peter to him? Cornelius needed to hear the whole counsel of God (Acts 20:27). He was living under the Old Testament, but there was a better way, grace and truth. Therefore, God sent Peter to share the good news about Jesus's death, burial, and resurrection for the sins of the world (Romans 10:14). Cornelius heard this good news and believed the message. He and his household were baptized (Acts 10:44–48). Paul writes:

> But after that the kindness and love of God our Savior toward man appeared. Not by works of righteousness which we have done, but according to his mercy he saved us, by the washing of regeneration, and renewing of the Holy Ghost (Titus 3:5).

Events exist or stay in your life for a short time. You are here today and gone tomorrow. Don't get comfortable with this life. The old spiritual song says, "We are just passing through." Thus, many events you didn't consider or anticipate will happen in your life. Illnesses will move from one part of the body to another, and you will notice physical and psychological changes. No longer will you do the things you did ten years or even two days ago. Your children, along with the neighborhood progenies, will grow up. Hence, the cares of this temporary life will begin to seem meaningless. Your priorities will change, and you will find yourself creating your last will and testament, putting monies away for the grandchildren, and reviewing your bucket list to determine which things you want to accomplish before you expire. Prepare to meet God because you are here today and perhaps gone tomorrow.

The Dash

When my dad purchased his tombstone, I thought it was premature. I surmise he wanted to ensure the writing on the slab of stone was to his liking. He had it prestamped with the day he was born, and next to that date was a dash. The dash is a small rectangle symbol that represents your entire life; nothing extra added, just a dash. No additional room to converse about what you did with your life. No regard to accomplishments, joys, or heartaches you endured. No mention of your walk with the Lord.

Obituaries begins with two dates and a dash in the middle. What people normally do upon hearing of your death is calculate your age. Then they shake their heads and think, *Too young to die.* Next, the cause of death inquiry comes. How you died causes others to ensure they don't die of the same thing. Well wishes to the family follow. Prior to lowering you in the ground, many testify about your life. But any amount of accomplishments achieved without the Lord amount to a wasted life. Solomon came to the same conclusion: "I have seen all the works that are done under the sun; and, behold; all is vanity and vexation of the spirit" (Ecclesiastes 1:9). He made that bold statement because he experienced it all: women, houses, land, money, fame, and power. Solomon looked over his entire life and concluded it was worthless without God.

Make your dash meaningful by living a godly life starting right now. Let your light shine before men (Matthew 5:16). After all, what truly matters in the end is your soul's destiny, not the dash. No one can create your dash for you. Create it for yourself by living for God. The Holy Spirit will help you. Jesus is your bridge to a fulfilled life. Your life will never mean much if you don't maintain a spiritual balance. Let your life be attractive enough that others are drawn to it.

Let your life mean more than just a dash.

Nothing on Earth Last Forever

Glaring down into a six-foot empty hole was an inverted hook device held up by four poles. The pallbearers carried the casket and placed it on the lowering device over the grave and lowered the casket. Rose petals tossed on top of the casket made their way downward in a spiral and cascading manner, landing on top of the brown-glazed burial box. Grandmother held my hand tightly with her left hand as she wiped her tears with the handkerchief in her right hand. Others stood about with bowed heads while the preacher tossed dirt into the open hole and his voice resounded, "Ashes to ashes, dust to dust." My mother's hammered, beaten body was lain to rest.

If you haven't noticed, nothing on earth last forever. Life ends when it ends. However, you can rest assured that you are in capable hands when it does. Jesus holds the keys of death (Revelation 1:18). Events occur and change without notification. Apples rot, trees fall, people die, money ceases, love fades, and relationships ends—none of which you can control. Change is both constant and vacillating, just like relationships. They begin, endure obstacles, and end. God is all about order, and a time is set in motion for all things to begin and end (1 Corinthians 14:40). In Ecclesiastes 3, Solomon states, "For everything there is a season, and a time for every matter under heaven." There is:

a time to be born and a time to die;

a time to plant, and a time to pluck up what is planted;

a time to kill, and a time to heal;

a time to break down, and a time to build up;

a time to weep, and a time to laugh;

a time to mourn, and a time to dance;

a time to cast away stones, and a time to gather stones together;

a time to embrace, and a time to refrain from embracing;

a time to seek, and a time to lose;

a time to keep, and a time to cast away;

a time to tear, and a time to sew;

a time to keep silence, and a time to speak;

a time to love, and a time to hate;

a time for war, and a time for peace.

The Old Testament is full of life changing stories. For instance, Joseph jealous brothers sold him into slavery. The children of Israel lived in a land that was undergoing a famine (Genesis 47:13). God used the evilness of Joseph's brothers to save a generation of people from starvation. He allowed Joseph's captivity into servitude for the very purpose to raise him up to become Pharaoh's second-in-command. Due to God's foresight, His people were save from starvation.

That's how God operates, in stealth mode. He plants someone in your path to encourage and help you along life's narrow way. The story doesn't end there. God's people prospered in Egypt (Genesis 47:20). Years later, Joseph died and a different Egyptian leader came into power (Exodus 1:8). God's people that were saved from starvation through Joseph's leadership were enslaved and stuck in Egypt for over four hundred years. The people must have thought their slavery would never end, but it did. It took them 430 years to come out of Egypt (Exodus 12:40). Think about it, four hundred years of servitude! Can you imagine your trials lasting that long?

Has God delivered you from life's circumstances at a moment when you thought all hope was lost? You may feel like you are stuck in your situation of financial instability, unemployment, and sickness. You may even think God is not listening to your prayers. Whatever you are experiencing, it won't last as it didn't last for the Israelites.

God is bigger than any circumstance that consume you. Don't let situations overshadow you into thinking there's no hope. Hope is all around you, even in death.

Apply your heart unto wisdom every moment and in all areas of your life (Psalm 90:12). Seek the Lord in all His ways (Proverbs 1:7). The beginning of wisdom is to recognize God and His power. Understanding that wisdom leads you to live a righteous life. Your soul will return to God who gave it (Ecclesiastes 12:7). Eternity will outlast this life.

One Chance

What comes to mind when you consider death? When I ponder death, I recognize I have one chance to get closer to God before entering into eternity. Death happens fast. A great example is a head-on car collision in which death is instantaneous. You weren't expecting it, and it occurred suddenly. Paul uses the verbiage "in the twinkling of an eye" to describe just how fast death occurs and how fast eternity becomes a reality. Once the transition takes place, there's no do-over. It's your final curtain call. In most cases, no notice or warning sign is given. That's scary!

What you see and feel right now is temporary. Death is a reality we can see and experience through each other's demise. Jesus gives a glimpse of death's reality in the story of the rich man and Lazarus (Luke 16:19-31). In the story, there was rich man who lived in luxury while Lazarus, a poor man, lived the life of a homeless man. The scriptures state that the rich man "fared sumptuously every day," which tells us he could have fed Lazarus but neglected to do so. The Bible says the dogs were more gracious to the beggar than the millionaire (Luke 16:21).

Both Lazarus and the rich man died (Luke 16:22). The rich man opened his reality eyes in torment, while Lazarus opened his reality eyes in paradise. Satan gives the illusion that this life is all you have and makes it pleasurable, irresistible, alluring, and real. He tells you to indulge and bask yourself in his reality. Satan keeps you in an aphrodisiac state so you won't consider your eternity. He is so bold as to tell you there's no hell, and when you die, you are just dead— that nothing happens to you in the grave. Other times he gets you involved in meaningless activities to keep your attention long enough so you won't notice your time winding down. If you truly knew there were no breaks, rests, or timeouts in hell, you would seriously take a look at eternality and change your ways.

The mere fact that the devil doesn't want you to live for Jesus is because he knows he's hell bound and wants your soul there too. What are you doing with the one shot you have? Let's put it this way: If you had to shoot a basketball in the game of life and had only one shot to do it, how would you play the game? Would you get in as much practice in godly living, or would you wait until test day, say a prayer, and hope for the best? Let's say sinking the ball into the hoop grants you entry into heaven; however, missing the hoop sends you to hell. Now, how would you play the game? Miss it and receive eternal torment or hoop it and receive eternal life. The caveat is that you don't know when your slide into eternity will occur.

My suggestion is for you to stand at the free throw line and carefully prepare and determine your shot.

> Wherefore, my beloved, as ye have always obeyed, not as in my presence only, but now much more in my absence, work out your own salvation with fear and trembling (Philippians 2:12).

> Teaching us that, denying ungodliness and worldly lusts, we should live soberly, righteously and godly in this present world (Titus 2:12).

The best way to get to paradise is to repent. Keep your future before you—your real future. Never forget God. Don't lose faith. Temptation and lust tend to make you forget you are on a journey that will end in heaven or hell. Learn obedience by the things you suffer, like Christ did (Hebrews 5:8). Your life troubles, whether you caused them or not, won't last, you do … on into eternity.

Edge of Eternity

Many of God's people are living on the edge of eternity right now and need to consider their ways (Haggai 1:7). The Bible speaks about a group of people who were close to claiming their reward. However, disobedience and complaining kept many of them from the promise. In Exodus 16:3, after God delivered His people from Egypt, and while holding their hands sojourning to the Promised Land, His people began to complain about their condition in the desert. They'd rather travel back to Egypt and be abused by their oppressors than go forward with God (Exodus 1:13–16). *Do you find yourself looking back because the travel forward seems difficult?*

Instead of thanking God for providing for their needs, the Israelites complained about what they didn't have. *When trying times occur, do you complain instead of counting your blessings?* It's easier to complain than to give thanks. Stop magnifying your unfortunate circumstances; rather, magnify the God you serve.

Learned lessons from the Bible:

1. You are on your way to the Promised Land, but you look back at your old life. Many of God's people talk about where they have been, but they have no idea where they are going. Satan wants you to remember the bad stuff: your illicit sexual encounters, your drug addictions, your hatred of others, your loose dressing, your foul mouth. He makes looking back memorable. It's time to stop looking at the past and walk forward into your new life. No matter how many times people bring up your past, you continue to march forward. Those same people will one day be led to Christ by your life.

   Therefore, if any man be in Christ, he is a new creature; old things are passed away; behold, all things are become new (2 Corinthians 5:17).

2. Stop fighting your brothers and sisters in the Lord. Jesus says, "Where there are two or three gathered in my name, there am I in the midst" (Matthew 18:20). If you work together, the church outreach program can bring many souls to the Lord. Fighting one another is a tool of the devil. He is a

master in the art of divide and conqueror. Stop acting like a child of God and be one.

Behold, how good and how pleasant it is for brethren
to dwell together in unity (Psalm 133:1).

3. You'd rather run away than stand for what you believe. An old proverb says something to the effect that you will fall for everything if you don't stand for something. Stand tall for Jesus. Refuse to be among the status quo; make a difference in a world full of darkness.

Let your light so shine before men that they may see
your good works, and glorify your Father which is in
heaven (Matthew 5:16).

4. You may feel God owes you something. God has done all He is going to do for you. He isn't going to give you anything that is in your control. You'll access what you need by faith (Romans 5:2). You'll experience God's goodness when you activate your faith. Your faith is not faith until it's all you've got to hold on to.

That ye be not slothful, but followers of them who
through faith and patience inherit the promises
(Hebrews 6:12).

For by grace are ye saved through faith; and that not
of yourselves; it's the gift of God (Ephesians 2:8).

The Great Reunion

There's a large group of God's people who are cheering you on right now and can't wait to share in your eternal joy when you get to heaven (Hebrews 12:1). Heaven is a place of praise and thanksgiving. Jesus will be the guest of honor. Like most parties, many people are fashionably late. At this gathering, everyone will be on time (Hebrews 9:27). Admission is free, thanks to Jesus's death on the cross (John 3:16). All who repented every chance they got and lived righteously will be there (Matthew 7:21). The attire will be crowns and robes. Refreshments will be bread and something Jesus calls "living water," followed by an out-of-this-world meal—oh boy!

Unlike most gatherings, no one needs to bring a gift. Heaven has everything you will need. The entertainment will be singing, joy, and praise. There will be real happiness and peace in that eternal spot. Start reserving your spot now. Jesus needs to know if you are trying to make an effort to be there so He can reserve a spot for you at His table. His invitation list, the Book of Life, is being compiled right now. Will He see you there? Of course if you don't know where you are going, any road will get you to hell. Choose your path wisely.

Forever Vacation Spot

If you want to go to heaven, start packing your bags for your forever vacation spot called eternity. I'm not advocating suicide; I'm promoting hope in the resurrected Lord on that final day—a day already paid for through Jesus's blood. His blood bought your ticket that's reserved in heaven at the registration booth. It's a one-way ticket with all expenses paid for an eternity of joy. No strings attached. You will dine at the finest table and meet biblical celebrities. You will walk streets paved with gold and live in a ten-star mansion overlooking heaven. All you have to do is open the door. Jesus is standing and knocking (Revelation 3:20). Notice, Jesus is standing at the door knocking. He is not forcing His way in, but waiting patiently for you to open your heart. Give your life to the one who died for you, and start earning blessings on your Christian frequent miles.

This offer is only good for the living. You've made financial plans for your children and grandchildren. Why not make plans for your eternal resting place? Book your next cruise with Jesus on the fantastic voyage cruise liner before it's too late. Such a simple request. Stop focusing on sin and the circumstances surrounding you, and walk your journey by faith.

Before you can experience the joys of heaven, you must die to self. Even a seed planted in soil must die first before it produces fruit (Luke 8:4–8), so shall it be with you when you die to self (Romans 8:31). You will flourish into a Christlike believer, if you're not already one. Rid yourself of things that keep you shackled to sin. Focus on what the Lord would have you do. Let your old self die and live your new life, which is a one-time event and a lifelong process. In other words, don't give up.

This temporary life won't last, you as a Child of God will on into eternity.

If you are reading this book and not a child of God, talk to God about your guilt and regrets. Ask for His forgiveness. Jesus died for your sins. This is the good news (1 Corinthians 15:3–4). Believe the good news (John 8:24) and repent of your sins before it's too late (Luke 3:3–5). Next, confess that Jesus is the Son of God—many in Jesus's day wouldn't do this for fear of being thrown out the synagogues (John 12:42). Then, be baptized as the three thousand were on the day of Pentecost (Act 2:37–46). Live as the first-century Christians did, and follow the apostles' teachings handed down from Jesus (1 Corinthians 11:1). Don't wait too long. For you who are a child of God, if you've taken a wrong turn in life, repent and ask the Father to forgive you. Get back on track. If not, your punishment will be worse than that of a person that doesn't know God.

> And that servant, which knew his lord's will, and prepared not himself, neither did according to his will, shall be beaten with many strips (Luke 12:47).

Remember, troubles don't last, you do!

About the Author

Kitt Swanson is a native of Syracuse, New York. At the early age of three years old she experienced the worst tragedy imaginable: she witnessed the murder of her mother. At the age of fourteen she found Christ while pondering suicide. She found her biological father eighteen years later. She knows what it is to be abased and to be bound. She has experienced heartaches, disappointments, and depression. She comforts the weary with the comfort she received from God. Through all her struggles, she is able to encourage others to keep reaching for heaven. She is an inspiration to all. She has twins named Jeremiah and Nehemiah and a cat named Koby.

To contact the author write:

Kitt Swanson

Kitt33604@yahoo.com

Printed in the United States
By Bookmasters